Power**Patter**

PowerPatter

More Than Just a Script Book for Hypnotists

Drake Eastburn, BCH, CI

Create Space Independent Publishing

Eastburn Hypnotherapy Center
Denver, CO
303-424-2331
www.hypnodenver.com
office@hypndenver.com

Contents

Contents

Contents

Acknowledgments

I can't say enough about my lovely wife, Lynsi Eastburn. Our coming together was due to some universal kismet. We met at an NGH (National Guild of Hypnotists) convention in 1999. Lynsi is from Canada and was living in Chicago at the time, while I was living in the Denver area. Dating over that distance was difficult and we both realized where this was going. So, after knowing each other for less than three months, we rushed off to Las Vegas to get married. We joke that we got married first and then started dating.

Lynsi was eager to become involved in the business, but my concern was that we first focus on our romantic life and then work on the business. I think we have managed to do just that. Being married as hypnotherapists has offered some advantages for us. Even though it has been a bumpy ride, we have managed to smooth out the road as we continue to become closer with each day.

Lynsi has done a lot of editing for me and having her around to consult with has been a real gift. Our two sons, Kelly and Dylan, have become hypnotists in their own right. Being surrounded by Lynsi and me has influenced them, and the boys have participated in a number of hypnosis related events and classes.

I would also like to acknowledge all of my students. They have encouraged me to put a lot of my words in writing and we have all benefited as a result. In fact, Eastburn Institute of Hypnosis only came into existence because of their insistence.

Martie O'Brien helped me out greatly with her skills in graphics and editing.

My good friend, Anita DiStefano, has done the typesetting on this book, as well as my previous book, *The Power of the Past.* If someone out there is writing a book and needs a good typesetter, then Anita is a great choice: *anita_d@mac.com.*

Introduction

Perhaps you are a hypnotist who has script books in your office. Perhaps you have scripts that you received during your training or from various classes that you may have attended. You may rely heavily on some of these scripts, while others you may never use at all. For the beginning hypnotist, scripts are the support system that can help one deal with whatever situation he or she might be confronted with. Certainly, as neophytes we all must start somewhere. Hopefully, after using scripts for a while, each hypnotist will rely on them less and less, beginning to develop his or her own language and starting to create the ability to work off the top of his or her head when necessary.

Personally, I have relied on scripts very little throughout my career in hypnosis. Early on, I picked up on language skills and was able to create my own patter as I went along. Eventually, I wrote down a lot of the verbiage that was working really well and shared it with my students and others. This verbiage is now the basis for this book.

I do own a lot of script books and every hypnotist should have a good selection of them. I have found a few scripts that I have used over and over again. Most script books, though, may have some really good scripts, but the rest is just filler. I have found some scripts to be downright bad. There have been times when it seemed to me that the author didn't have a script for a particular issue, so he or she just sat down at the keyboard and pounded one out without really testing it out ahead of time.

I refer to the script books that I have fairly often. I don't necessarily use the scripts, but I will often find that there is an idea or a sentence in the script that works really well, and I can insert it into whatever I am doing.

At Eastburn Hypnotherapy Center there are some scripts that get used a lot. "The Gray Room" is a script that we received from Jerry Kein and Steven Parkhill, although I'm not sure of its origin. Roy Hunter's "Mental Confusion" script gets a lot of airplay as well. I have recommended Carol Summers's book, *Conversational Hypnosis*, to my students. Her book is Ericksonian based, and has a very good repertoire of suggestions that is very similar to what I've been teaching my students for a long time. It's nice to see a hypnotist who knows what an embedded suggestion is and is not afraid to use it.

I am not giving you a large book full of patter that will fit every possible issue that might come walking into your office. I am giving you some patter that I have used over and over again and has been tested out by myself, my students and other therapists working at Eastburn Hypnotherapy Center. Some of these scripts are adaptable to a great number of issues and have worked well for me over the years. If you were to memorize just a few of these scripts, you would be well prepared no matter what issue might pop up. Some are very unique and powerful.

I would like to say that anyone who used one of my scripts would have 100 percent success, but we know that hypnosis is not like that. If it were simply the words in a given script that made all of the difference, then there would be no need to seek training as a hypnotist—anyone could just read out of a book. It's more than just the words written on the paper. It has to do with the hypnotist's abilities and how the voice is used. It also has to do with the intake leading up to the hypnosis session and the waking hypnosis. What is said to the client prior to the trance piece will help to create success with much of the patter in this book. I will spend some time explaining the patter and how to use it, so that you can gain the best results.

There is an additional copy of each script at the back of the book for your convenience. This way they are all in one place so you can access them quickly without having to search for them in their individual chapters.

Many times I have had clients come into my office and complain that they saw some other hypnotist who just sat there and read to them from a book. It would be unreasonable to think that a hypnotist could possibly memorize every possible script that they might need for any situation. However, it's not hard to understand how a client, who doesn't know about hypnosis, might lose some confidence when they see the hypnotist reading from a book. Usually your clients will have their eyes closed and won't be aware if you're reading parts of their session. Keep any printed materials that you will use out of sight. Avoid rattling any pages (clients will notice this). Put any scripts that you use frequently in sheet protectors. This not only serves to keep your valuable materials safe; it also eliminates the paper noise.

If I have a script that's more than one page of copy, I insert the first page and second page on separate pieces of paper into the same sheet protector. This method uses more paper, but it adds some substance and makes the script easier to handle. If you have a script that is long enough that it requires several sheet protectors, put a ring binder through the sheets to keep the sheets in order. This will save you from having to shuffle through the papers to find the right order, and will keep you from accidentally reading the wrong page. If you know you will be using a certain script, then stick it under the edge of the client's recliner where you can access it after the trance induction.

Keep your favorite scripts organized so that you can access them quickly when you need to. It's also a good idea to make extra copies of those that you use frequently, just to be sure they are always on hand.

Never, never, ever use a script in a session that you have not previously familiarized yourself with. You could end up doing something very embarrassing, or even worse. Also, get to know your client during the intake. That script that just worked an hour ago for someone with the same issue may be totally inappropriate for the next client.

I ask that you don't share these scripts with others. It's not that I'm selfish or afraid that I won't make a dollar because someone got a script for free. My concern is that unless they have read *Power Patter* or taken my training, they won't have a proper understanding of how to use these scripts. As a result, they may not use the scripts to the fullest benefit.

Most of the scripts that I offer here are not intended to stand alone. Usually I include scripts together or use other direct suggestions along with them.

You will find a number of scripts that deal with weight loss. It wouldn't take much to take these scripts and some of your own knowledge and use them to put together a weight loss program of your own.

Some of the scripts deal with smoking or could easily be adapted for work with smoking. If you have already been trained to work with smokers and are doing pretty well in that area, then, by all means, use these scripts. If you have not had advanced training in working with smokers, then get that training. Oftentimes a hypnotist's foundational training isn't enough to be good at working with smokers. If all you got were some scripts to read and no further training, then you are not doing enough for smokers. If you or your instructor does not feel confident doing smokers in a single session, then, in my opinion, it is important to do whatever it takes to get there. My own "Puffed Enuff" class is an extensive weekend class in working with smoking and other addictions that I have been teaching internationally for years. Jerry Kein teaches single-session-stop-smoking as well and there are certainly others. I believe that every hypnotist needs to be able to do single-session-stop-smoking.

A Bad Script Example

Some years back, I was teaching the part of hypnosis training dealing with suggestion work. I decided to bring in an example of a bad script so that everyone could understand the pitfalls of simply grabbing an unfamiliar script for a particular issue and just reading it to a client. I pulled a script book off my shelf and it fell open to a script that I thought was perfect for my example. I have used this script as an example with every class I have taught since. This script deals with grief, and the person who wrote the script did have some training in this area. However, transferring that knowledge into a hypnosis script didn't work out so well. This script was intended by the author to be tape-recorded and listened to over and over. An excerpt from it should give you an idea of why I refer to it as the "Bad Script." Most of the students who have read the script only got part way through it and put it down.

> Someone you have dearly loved has died. You feel a sense of emptiness and void. You have flashing ideas that at any moment your loved one will walk through the door or call on the telephone. You bounce like a rubber ball between shock and denial. There is an ache and terror of loneliness.

Well, if we weren't already feeling the shock and ache and terror of loneliness, we are now, and we only had to read the first four sentences to get there. Continuing on with this script doesn't improve the situation at all. The author of this script must never have heard about avoiding painted words. Painted words are those words which contain the very thing we are trying to get away from, such as; *pain, grief, terror, fear, loneliness, heartache* and the like. When we hear these words, they bring our attention right to the very thing we are trying to get away from, and we generate the feelings associated with them.

The author of the "Bad Script" goes on to bring his own religious beliefs into the script. Never, never assume that your religious views are what are accepted by everyone. This particular author would probably not appreciate someone reading a script to him insinuating that Allah or Mohammed is here to cure his problems, and he should not impose his beliefs on someone else. If you have a client who has strong religious leanings, then you could make use of that resource. It's very shaky ground to arbitrarily put something of a religious nature into a script.

As hypnotists or therapists, the first thing on our agenda should be to do no harm. It is possible that reading a script like this to someone could make things worse than they were to start with. Certainly, listening to this script on a tape over and over again, as it was intended, would be horrible.

The No Suggestion Suggestion 2

The No Suggestion Suggestion is probably the most powerful script I can give you. If there is one script that you should definitely have in your memory, this is it.

I developed this script many years ago as a result of a phenomenon that I had witnessed many times. If you have worked with many clients yourself then you have probably noticed this same thing. The phenomenon is that clients will often give themselves whatever suggestion it is that they need at the time. That is to say that, regardless of the words that come out of the therapist's mouth, the client gets out of his or her session whatever it was that they really needed, even if that wasn't made apparent during the intake portion.

I've often had clients sit up at the conclusion of their session and say excitedly, "You know it was that suggestion about [*such and such*] that really hit home with me." Of course, being a good hypnotist, I agree enthusiastically with my client, all the time knowing that I never said such a thing at all.

It seemed that my client's own subconscious mind knew what they were in need of and just created it in the session without my involvement. I had one young man sit up after his session and declare enthusiastically that it was the Reiki that I had performed during the trance that caused his transformation. Again, I agreed wholeheartedly with client, saying, "Yes, isn't it just amazing!" Of course, I didn't let on that at that time I didn't have a clue what Reiki was. However, I did know about hypnosis, and I knew that it had just worked on him no matter what name he put to it.

I was involved in a demonstration for training purposes in which another hypnotherapist was leading a session and several students were sitting around as observers. At the end of the session the student client sat up and declared that it was such and such that the trainer had said that had this amazing impact on her. People who were observing the session began looking at each other blankly, because they all knew that no such thing had been said during her session. I had noticed this phenomenon occur more and more in my practice and I wanted to take better advantage of it.

I never sat down to write out the No Suggestion Suggestion. Bits just started popping into my head as I worked with clients, and I was getting some really amazing results. When I first began using this piece, a woman came to me who had fibromyalgia and chronic fatigue syndrome. We had several conversations over the phone and she had sent her husband to see me (most likely to find out if it was safe or not). After he had success, she decided she could finally try a session herself.

This woman had set a number of appointments with me and had canceled due to the pain of the fibromyalgia. She was a very large woman and even her clothes rubbing against her body would cause her a great deal of discomfort. She wouldn't drive because that increased her discomfort and her mother or husband would drive her. I didn't generally see clients in my home, but she lived nearby and wanted to see me at home. The house that I was in at the time had a very long steep set of stairs leading to the front door. It took this woman a long time just to negotiate those stairs.

During the intake portion of her session, I found that she had an extensive history of health issues and abuse. The intake had ended up being lengthy and there wasn't a lot of time left to complete the session. I quickly got her into somnambulism and I used the No Suggestion Suggestion. On emerging at the end of the session, the woman sat up and looked me in the eye and said, "You are good; you are really good." She said, "I knew I was going to remember that suggestion, but you did it. I can't remember what it was."

As the woman began to gather up her possessions to leave, I noticed that she was moving about quite freely and easily (much different from the restrained painful motions when she came in). I commented on her movement and she exclaimed, "Yes, look at me, look at me," as she danced about the room. I watched her as she literally bounced down the stairs when she left (the same stairs which had been such a formidable obstacle on her arrival). Her mother was watching from the car at the bottom of the stairs as my client bounced around the driveway exclaiming, "Look at me, look at me!" I was left feeling like some faith healer and knowing that I was on the right track.

Since then I have used the No Suggestion Suggestion many thousands of times. I have often advised my students that, when unsure of what to do, use the No Suggestion Suggestion. It's hard to go wrong with that. The worst thing that could happen is that the client just gets a lot of positive encouragement.

The wording of the No Suggestion Suggestion is more personalized and therefore is more applicable to individuals than groups. I do, however, use it in small groups, especially those in which the individuals are known to each other. Often, small groups of smokers or weight people are friends or family members, and this makes it easier to keep the wording more personal. Additionally, the wording is intended to make the clients feel special, as if they may possess some special quality that makes them good candidates for this piece.

With the No Suggestion Suggestion, the therapist is creating the expectancy that the client is going to receive some very special, very powerful suggestion that has a unique side effect: They will not be able to remember this very special suggestion. Of course, if the client's conscious mind is at all present, then the words *side effect* will get its attention, and this only helps to suck the mind into the process. During the patter, the therapist is telling the client that he or she is going to receive a suggestion that the client won't even remember and that very few people have ever received. During this time the therapist is giving one suggestion after the other.

In one sense, there is no No Suggestion Suggestion, but in the other sense they *are* getting that one very special, very powerful suggestion that is unique to that client, because we are giving them the opportunity to create that suggestion for themselves. What could be more unique or personal than that?

I have had many clients whom I saw years after they were given the No Suggestion Suggestion and they would ask me about it. I've had some clients who became students later on and just lost it when they found out in class what it's all about.

I also use some other patter with the No Suggestion Suggestion. One is the No Suggestion Follow-Up, which is used at the end the session. It helps to set the suggestion in the mind and create greater expectancy. The other is the No Suggestion Connect. This patter is used only in a following session with someone who has previously received the No Suggestion Suggestion. That next session could be a week or months or even years later.

The No Suggestion Suggestion is not meant to stand alone. It works best with some other patter before and after. That patter might be just some direct suggestions off the top of your head or some other scripts that you are familiar with.

The first script is the No Suggestion Suggestion in a form that can be adapted to a lot of different situations. Then you will find the No Suggestion Suggestion as I use it during a smoking session. Whichever patter you use, end your session with the No Suggestion Follow-Up. The No Suggestion Follow-Up is then followed by the No Suggestion Connect, which is only to be used in some later session.

Note: It is assumed that, during the intake, the hypnotist has explained to the client the difference between the conscious and the subconscious mind. If you haven't been doing that already, then you will need to start now.

The No Suggestion Suggestion Script

At some point I'm going to be giving you a suggestion. At some point I'm going to be giving you a suggestion, a very special, a very powerful suggestion, so powerful in fact that this suggestion is effective one hundred percent of the time. Very few people have ever received this very special, very powerful suggestion. However, because of some of the things that you said during the interview process, I now know that you are ready, willing, and able to receive this suggestion, fully and completely, body, mind and spirit. *Now,* there is a side effect to this suggestion, and that side effect is that you won't even remember this suggestion. It doesn't matter that you won't remember this suggestion, because I'm going to slip in this suggestion in such a way that you won't even notice it. It doesn't matter that you won't remember this suggestion because your subconscious mind knows this suggestion. Yes, your subconscious mind knows this suggestion and your subconscious mind enjoys this suggestion. And because your subconscious mind enjoys this suggestion, your subconscious mind embraces this suggestion. Because your subconscious mind embraces this suggestion, good, healthy, positive changes occur in your life, not the least of which is [*insert client specifics here, such as,* "you are a non-smoker for the rest of your life," *or,* "you are free of that unwanted emotional baggage," *or,* "you have greater confidence," *or you can even leave it unspecified*], all because of this one very special, very powerful suggestion that I'm going to give you at some point, that you won't even remember.

Now, other good, healthy, positive changes will occur as well, all because of this one very special, very powerful suggestion and something I refer to as the domino effect. Yes, any time we take control in our lives just as you are doing right this very moment by [*insert client specifics here, or say nothing at all*], it's as if you are knocking over that first domino and the rest of the dominos begin to topple and other good, healthy, positive changes begin to fall right into your life. Some of these good, healthy, positive changes will be fairly obvious like [*client specific, or not*]. You have a great deal more energy. You feel like doing more vigorous, more active kinds of things and you do do more vigorous, more active kinds of things. You think more clearly. You have a new, more positive attitude, a new optimism; you're always looking ahead to each new day, knowing that good things are coming your way. You blaze the trail for others to follow. Yes, you set the example that others follow.

Now, other good, healthy, positive changes will occur as well, and I'm not even sure what some of these changes might be. I'd only be speculating and most likely so would you. However, it's nice to know that the subconscious mind knows exactly which good, healthy, positive changes you're up for and in what order they need to occur. It's nice to know that consciously there's not much you need to think about. There's not much you need to do. It's nice to know that the subconscious mind just takes care of everything.

Now, some of these changes may occur on a fairly subtle level. And you may be someone who is aware on a subtle level, or perhaps the hypnosis helps you to be more aware on a subtle level; it really doesn't matter at all. As you may know, sometimes things that occur on a subtle level have a very profound effect upon us—body, mind and spirit. All because of this one very special, very powerful suggestion and the domino effect.

THE NO SUGGESTION SUGGESTION SCRIPT
(SMOKING)

At some point I'm going to be giving you a suggestion. At some point I'm going to be giving you a suggestion, a very special, a very powerful suggestion, so powerful in fact that this suggestion is effective one hundred percent of the time. Very few people have ever received this very special, very powerful suggestion. However, because of some of the things that you said during the interview process, I now know that you are ready, willing and able to receive this suggestion, fully and completely, body, mind and spirit. *Now,* there is a side effect to this suggestion, and that side effect is that you won't even remember this suggestion. It doesn't matter that you won't remember this suggestion, because I'm going to slip in this suggestion in such a way that you won't even notice it. It doesn't matter that you won't remember this suggestion because your subconscious mind knows this suggestion. Yes, your subconscious mind knows this suggestion and your subconscious mind enjoys this suggestion. And because your subconscious mind enjoys this suggestion, your subconscious mind embraces this suggestion. Because your subconscious mind embraces this suggestion, good, healthy, positive changes occur in your life, not the least of which is the fact that you are a non-smoker for the rest of your life, never again desiring cigarettes or tobacco in any form. All because of this one very special, very powerful suggestion that I'm going to give you at some point, that you won't even remember.

Now, other good, healthy, positive changes will occur as well, all because of this one very special, very powerful suggestion and something I refer to as the domino effect. Yes, any time we take control in our lives just as you are doing right this very moment by becoming a non-smoker for the rest of your life, it's as if you are knocking over that first domino and the rest of the dominos begin to topple and other good, healthy, positive changes begin to fall right into your life. Some of these good, healthy, positive changes will be fairly obvious, like you are a non-smoker for the rest of your life. You breathe more easily. You feel better about yourself and who you are. You have a great deal more energy. You feel like doing more vigorous, more active kinds of things and you do do more vigorous, more active kinds of things. You think more clearly. You have a new, more positive attitude, a new optimism;

you're always looking ahead to each new day, knowing that good things are coming your way. You blaze the trail for others to follow. Yes, you set the example that others follow.

Now, other good, healthy, positive changes will occur as well. Some of these changes may or may not have anything to do with being a non-smoker and I'm not even sure what some of these changes might be. I'd only be speculating and most likely so would you. However, it's nice to know that the subconscious mind knows exactly which good, healthy, positive changes you're up for and in what order they need to occur. It's nice to know that consciously there's not much you need to think about. There's not much you need to do. It's nice to know that the subconscious mind just takes care of everything and good, healthy, positive changes come to you.

Now, some of these changes may occur on a fairly subtle level. And you may be someone who is aware on a subtle level, or perhaps the hypnosis helps you to be more aware on a subtle level; it really doesn't matter at all. As you may know, sometimes things that occur on a sub-tle level have a very profound effect upon us, body, mind and spirit. All because of this one very special, very powerful suggestion and the domino effect.

As a result, your new non-smoking lifestyle becomes a compulsion for you. Not only are you a non-smoker, you take control of your life in other ways as well—like the kinds of nutrients you put in your body. You know the value of maintaining a healthy diet and in the proper quan-tities. Exercise is a similar kind of thing. You know the value of living an active lifestyle. And now as a non-smoker you have a great deal more energy and you feel like doing more vigorous, more active kinds of things, and you do do more vigorous, more active kinds of things.

You take time out for yourself as well—time to do your own things, time to have your own thoughts and feelings, time to just kick back and relax. And you're very relaxed right this very moment and you can only be this relaxed as a non-smoker. No one could be this relaxed and smoking at the same time, and you are this relaxed, and you are a non-smoker. And because you are this relaxed, all of the suggestions take complete and thorough effect upon you, body, mind and spirit.

THE NO SUGGESTION FOLLOW-UP SCRIPT

[You will give (read) this piece of patter to your client near the end of the session.]

You may remember any of this session you wish to remember, with the one exception of that one very special, very powerful suggestion that I gave you at some time that you won't even remember. It doesn't matter that you won't remember that suggestion, for it's the effects of that suggestion upon you that are important and the effects of that suggestion will follow you day by day, body, mind and spirit. Now, you might wonder about that suggestion. You might think about that suggestion. You may even try and remember that suggestion; however, it will just make the suggestion more powerful and you will still not be able to remember it.

THE NO SUGGESTION CONNECT SCRIPT

[Often, in following sessions, I use the No Suggestion Connect with a client who has previously been given the No Suggestion Suggestion. This could happen during the client's next session a week or so apart, or I've even used it months or years later. The wording is something like the following.]

The last time we were together, I gave you a suggestion, a very special suggestion. That suggestion has continued to work on you mind, body and spirit, and that's probably one reason why you are here today. Today, I'm going to give you another suggestion, a different suggestion, but a somewhat similar suggestion. Because I'll be giving you this suggestion now and because I gave you that suggestion then, both suggestions become more powerful than they could have ever become on their own. Sometimes adding one and one together ends up being a lot more than two, something I refer to as compounding, and both suggestions become many times more powerful than they ever could have on their own.

[Follow this with other suggestion work.]

Choices

The Choices script is one that I use a whole lot with my weight clients. It deals with diet and exercise, and deals a lot with eating out, which has become a bigger issue with our modern lifestyles. This script is encouraging clients to think outside the box.

The Choices Script

We live in a world of choices, and choices are a good thing. Choices are what give us freedom and the ability to be unique and creative individuals. Without choices we would all just be clones of one another.

When it comes to food and exercise there are lots and lots of choices we can make. Perhaps you find yourself going to restaurants or fast food places from time to time. When I was a youngster, going to a restaurant was a really big deal, because it happened so infrequently. So, of course, everyone wanted to order his or her favorites and get dessert if possible, because you never knew when that was going to happen again. Back then it probably wasn't such a big issue, because food was different and lifestyles were different and it happened so infrequently that it wasn't a big factor in our health. Nowadays, due to our speeded up hurry-here-hurry-there lifestyles, restaurants and fast food places have become more a part of our normal routines. We can no longer afford to treat each trip to a restaurant or fast food place as if it were a special occasion. Some restaurants have lots and lots of choices that we can make and usually this is a good thing. The more choices there are, the more opportunities there are to make good, healthy, intelligent choices. It feels good to make those good, healthy, intelligent choices that put you in control. At first it may seem a little strange eating so much differently than others around you, like people you might be dining with or just people sitting about the restaurant. But soon it seems strange to eat in any other way. Your positive eating choices help to influence others in a positive way as well. Other people begin to notice that you are eating differently. Not only do they notice that you are eating differently, they notice a difference in you, which may influence them to make better, healthier choices, as well.

Other people have what I refer to as that cattle herd mentality. In the cattle herd, that's where everyone just does the same things that everyone else does. Well, there may be some warm fuzzies in that, but when everyone does the same thing that everyone else does, then everyone gets pretty much the same results that everyone else gets, and when you look out there that can be pretty scary.

You, however, are someone who is willing to think outside of the box. You are someone who is willing to try something different. I know that because you are here today and that's the sort of action a person takes who's willing to think outside the box, and do something different. That's what people do who make a difference in their lives, a difference in the world. You make a difference by doing something different. Doing the same old things only gives the same results; it's only by doing something different that we can make a difference, a difference in our lives, a difference in the world. It feels good to make the good, healthy, intelligent choices that make a difference for you.

Some restaurants and fast food places have fewer choices than others; however, some choices are still better than others. It feels good to make the good, healthy, intelligent choices that put you in control. *Now*, at some restaurants and fast food places there may be so few choices or such poor choices that sometimes it's better to make no choice at all, than to make a poor choice. You know a poor choice could mean a setback and you avoid any type of setbacks, for you desire to keep moving ahead in a positive direction. And you know that somewhere, shortly down the road, there will be an opportunity to make good, healthy, intelligent choices that put you in control. It feels good to make the good, healthy, intelligent choices that put you in control.

The grocery store is another place where we get to make choices. At the grocery store there are lots and lots of choices that we could make. And this is a good thing, because the more choices there are, the more opportunities there are to make good, healthy, intelligent choices that put you in control. It feels good to make those good, healthy, intelligent choices that put you in control. There have been times when you were in the grocery store and you made some good, healthy, intelligent choices that put you in control and it feels good. You know what I mean. There have been times when you made good, healthy, intelligent choices that put you in control and it feels good. And when you make the good, healthy, intelligent choices that put you in control, you are in control. You are in control of your health. You are in control of your aliveness. You are in control of your body. You are in control of the way you look and feel. It feels good to make the good, healthy, intelligent choices that put you in control.

On the other hand, there have been times when you made a poor choice, and you knew you were making a poor choice. You made a poor choice; you knew it was a poor choice; yet you continued to make the poor choice. As a result you feel guilty, embarrassed, discouraged, disgusted, uncomfortable and out of control. You hate feeling out of control. You hate feeling uncomfortable, yet there you are. You made a poor choice; you knew it was a poor choice. As a result you feel guilty, embarrassed, discouraged, disgusted, uncomfortable and out of control. You hate feeling out of control. You hate feeling uncomfortable. As a result you can't even enjoy the poor choice. Yes, you've added insult to injury; you've poured salt in your own wound. You made a poor choice. You knew it was a poor choice. As a result you feel guilty, embarrassed, discouraged, disgusted, uncomfortable and out of control. These awful feelings and sensations take away from any enjoyment you might have gotten from that poor choice. Not only is there no enjoyment from that poor choice, you've wasted good money, and you put poison into your body. What could be worse than that? How awful is that?

From now on you can't even get near one of those poor choices without feeling guilty, embarrassed, discouraged, disgusted, uncomfortable and out of control. You hate feeling out of control. You hate feeling uncomfortable. There you are in the grocery store, pushing your cart down the aisle, and you're right near one of those poor choices. You can feel the guilty, embarrassing, discouraging, uncomfortable, out of control sensations gushing right up through your body. You feel guilty, embarrassed, discouraged, disgusted, uncomfortable, out of control. *It feels awful!* The best thing, the best thing that you can do, is to quickly move away, and quickly go make some good, healthy, positive, intelligent choices that put you in control. It feels good to make the good, healthy, positive, intelligent choices that put you in control. When you make the good, healthy, positive, intelligent choices that put you in control, you are in control. You are in control of your health; you are in control of your body. You are in control of the way you look and feel. It feels good to make the good, healthy, positive, intelligent choices that put you in control.

When it comes to exercise, there are lots and lots of good, healthy, positive, intelligent choices you can make. Some of these choices are simple little things you can do every day, like using the stairs instead of the elevator or escalator. Or park your car further away when you are at the grocery store or the shopping mall or at work. Not only is parking further away a simple way to add a little exercise into our daily routine, we are taking better care of our vehicle at the same time. And walk to the convenience store or other places instead of driving. Every little thing we do like this is helpful toward making us leaner and healthier. It feels good to make the good, healthy, intelligent choices that put you in control.

Chaos

4

Chaos is a script that I wrote shortly before Lynsi and I got married. I was flying to Chicago to see her for a couple of days. On the plane, I started coming up with this idea that was the basis of this script. I created about 90 percent of it on that flight and then I spent years refining it and adding the last few sentences.

Chaos is a weight script that relies heavily on embedded suggestions. I use this script a lot with groups and other weight clients. It works really well on those individuals who like to stay in their intellectual minds. The intellectual mind tries to follow along, because it seems that the script is making sense, but it never really gives the intellectual mind anything to hang on to. While the intellectual mind is busy trying to make sense of the verbiage, I'm busy slipping in suggestions.

This is the only script of mine that I actually read, and you can understand why once you read it. Pay attention to any words that are italicized, for these are the embedded suggestions. For an embedded suggestion to work you must change your tone or pause slightly.

Several years back, I had a participant who was a local psychologist in one of my weight groups. She never went into trance during the three-week program. She sat in her seat the entire time, writing down every word I said each evening. I suspected that she was creating her own weight group and was going to use my material. Towards the end of the last evening she was busy writing away during the trance piece. When I got into the Chaos script, I looked over and her pad and paper had fallen to the floor and she was out like a light.

After using this script, you might want to try developing your own script using the Chaos method.

THE CHAOS SCRIPT

In the southern central portion of the north mainly in the panhandle, it's about as round as a perfect square can be and still remain perpendicular. Up until then nothing was really normal except the sight of the air, when things were really noisy, and there was the crunching of numbers to cause consideration. It was easier to *let go of all that weight* and let it sink to the ceiling, like *in no time at all*. Only the ones with two or more on the left had a good sense of sideways. Mostly party members. Other joiners *become fit as well*. Meandering as if it were no effort at all. Even toppling upright seemed to have a positive effect. Especially during the night light or after. It was easier to *just lighten up*. No more sinking sensations. It only happened at those odd times anyway. So you have that to look forward to. Even though you may not remember when it finally does happen, isn't it strange when *it works* that way? So you have that to look forward to, even though you may not remember when it finally does happen. Isn't it strange when *it works* that way? There is no struggle of course when that does happen. And you *become firm* each time. You've had that happen before. I noticed that about you a number of times in the past when you thought no one was paying attention. You may have thought you weren't being noticed. Some certainly did not. It flows both ways, just like snow up the hill. On the other side it's smooth and you *become light on your feet* it's easier than carrying that weight up the hill. Soaking up the light sensations below. Afterwards it seems to make sense, especially the movement, you can't cross your legs in that position anyway it feels better to *stretch out first*. I learned that years before in adulthood. Funny how that could make sense and something about floating weightless happens even when *you try harder*. *You can be firm* about that most are. It happens when you most expect and sometimes more. There's no need to not wonder why. It crosses over into familiar territory, if you follow what I mean, not that I could ever be mean. It's just more comfortable to uncross legs sometimes. Other parts work easier this time of year as well and not just during the day. You've probably hovered around that issue a time or two. It can be good as things *change for the better*. What once weighed heavily now evaporates easily into thin. Most forms of transportation rarely do that, although *things can be different in the future*. They dug a big hole just to support the feeling light. It worked better than that old prop. Throats get dry that way and *action is necessary*. Who could foresee that? And not just in the suburbs if you know what I mean. It doesn't matter what the weather is doing, it's always a good time to—*do that*. It's nuts to think it couldn't *work out* just in that way. You're in control. I know that because you are here right now. How could it be different? Everyone else goes down that other stone road, just like it was a field. Some people learned it in school, you'll just have to ... Be smart enough ... to *do it on your own*. Midway between you get off way ahead, I couldn't tell you more. It seemed strange to me too until we ... *Find that change*— there's no substitute for that. You planted the seed, you know what is happening as *it dwindles away*. You may have had it happen before, just not as easily. It happens that way only *easier now*. That other time can just *let go now*. You have a mind of your own and no one else can change it. You already know what you want. You know what you will do. Even if for just 59 seconds anyone can do 59 seconds. You know you are just right *now*. It's the best time *now*. Later could be too late. It's never cloudy then. Only good happens *now*. What once was fuzzy and fluffy is now *firm and smooth*. Mostly there is no need to be too deep. It works well both ways. There's no time like the present regardless of what happened before. You're not the same person as then. *You have a mind of your own* and you have set it. It feels good to move from one thing to the next. *The body enjoys movement*. It's good to have those choices and there are lots of choices, *you know the right choices,* I don't even need to tell you that. It feels better to make the right choices. It takes such a weight off. It's just so much easier that way. Not like struggling the wrong way. That happened before, no longer. Mostly sunny now. You can see through the haze. The body enjoys feeling healthy. Outside and feel the light. *Light meals*. Whenever. You're going to be there anyway. It's barely abstract, bituminous perhaps. Some smaller cities are that way. One can only imagine. It's not to say it smelled some way or different all together. Whatever and whichever it doesn't seem to make any difference, each day is and every way things seem to work in your favor. No matter where you are or what you may be doing you find things *work in your favor*. It's nice to know wherever you are whatever you might be doing things are working in your favor; you have control of *feeling good about yourself*. No matter who might be around or what you might be doing, *it feels good to take care of yourself first*. You don't mind being different from others, that's how you make a difference in you.

Full

How do you know when you've had enough? This is a question I ask my weight loss clients. Usually, the answer is something like, "when I'm full," or, "when I'm stuffed." Some even say that they don't know when they have had enough—they can get full and just keep right on going.

Were you taught to clean your plate as a youngster? Sure, we belonged to the clean plate club. There are children starving in China, you know. We would have to sit there all night or we would have to finish it for breakfast the next morning and it was cold. Some were even beaten till they ate everything on their plate.

This is a huge problem in our society. We learned early on to override our normal sensations that tell us when we have had enough. Some people were then rewarded for overeating—when you finish that mound of road kill, then you can have dessert. So how does this work? If you are too full and you force yourself to overeat even more, then your reward will be *more food!* It's no wonder that weight is becoming such a huge issue in this country (pun intended).

Full is a script that helps us to get back in control of our natural appetite signals. This is a piece that has been a mainstay in my practice for some time. Use it early with your weight clients. Make it believable.

The Full Script

There have been times, everybody has had times. You have had times. I have had times. Everybody has had times, times when you've just had way, way, way too much. You know what I mean, times when you have just had way, way, way too much to eat. Perhaps there have been some family gatherings, like Thanksgiving or Christmas or a wedding reception, or some other celebration where there is just lots and lots of food—you know, what some people might refer to as a spread. I guess we've all had the feelings, sensations, ideas or thoughts that, wow, it all looks so good, I think I'll just try a little bit of everything. You know, by the time you've tried a little bit of everything, it's just way, way, way too much. You know what I mean. You probably find yourself drifting back to a particular incident where you've just had way, way, way too much to eat. You know how it feels. You can feel it in your body right this very moment. You feel full, stuffed, heavy, sluggish, slow, bloated and sloth-like. You hate feeling bloated; you hate feeling uncomfortable. You probably wonder why? Why did I ever think this was a good idea? You might wish you could turn back time, but you cannot. You feel full, stuffed, heavy, sluggish, slow, bloated and sloth-like. You hate feeling bloated, you hate feeling uncomfortable. One more bite, one more bite would be enough to put you over the edge, to cause you to explode, or become violently ill. You probably feel a bit nauseous right now. You feel full, stuffed, heavy, sluggish, slow, bloated and sloth-like. You hate feeling bloated; you hate feeling uncomfortable. You might feel a bit embarrassed; yes, your stomach is so pooched out there is nothing you can do to hide it, and who knows who might be noticing. You probably find yourself loosening your clothing a bit, trying to get some kind of relief, but even that doesn't help all that much. You feel full, stuffed, heavy, sluggish, slow, bloated and sloth-like. You hate feeling bloated; you hate feeling uncomfortable. You might notice that you have difficulty breathing. Yes, your stomach is so full that your diaphragm can no longer expand properly and all you get are these short little breaths of air. You might even feel a bit vulnerable. Yes, if there were some kind of an emergency, you don't know if you could move fast enough to save yourself, let alone help anyone else. All you really want to do is kick back and relax and wait for these awful feelings and sensations to go away, but it just takes forever. You feel full, stuffed, heavy, sluggish, slow, bloated and sloth-like. You hate feeling bloated; you hate feeling uncomfortable. You will do anything to avoid these awful feelings and sensations. From now on, you notice these sensations come on so much more quickly, so much more easily now. Sometimes all it takes is a bite or two or three and you feel full, stuffed, heavy, sluggish, slow, bloated and sloth-like. You hate feeling bloated; you hate feeling uncomfortable. You will do anything to avoid these awful feelings and sensations.

There are certain times when these awful feelings and sensations come on so much more quickly, so much more easily than before. For instance, perhaps you find yourself wandering into the kitchen when you're not even hungry. Perhaps you've eaten not that long ago, but there you are, poking through the cupboards or the refrigerator or the counters. You find yourself looking for that one little morsel that is going to make the world all right. From now on, all it takes is one little bite, one little cookie, one little cracker or potato chip, one little bite of chocolate or ice cream or candy or any sort of sweet or salty or fatty or carbohydratie or snacky item to put you right over the edge. To put you right into those full, stuffed, heavy, sluggish, slow, bloated and sloth-like sensations that you despise. You hate feeling bloated; you hate feeling uncomfortable; you'll do anything to avoid them. From now on, you can't even think about what might be in that kitchen when you're not hungry. You can't look in those cupboards or refrigerator without feeling full, stuffed, heavy, sluggish, slow, bloated and sloth-like. You hate feeling bloated; you hate feeling uncomfortable. You'll do anything to avoid these awful feelings and sensations. And the best thing that you can do to avoid these awful feelings and sensations is to eat very ... very ... slowly ... and cautiously. For you know how quickly, how easily, these full, stuffed, heavy, sluggish, slow, bloated and sloth-like sensations can come creeping up on you. You hate feeling bloated; you hate feeling uncomfortable. At the first sign, at the very first sign of any sensations of satisfaction, you discontinue eating. You push your plate away. You put your food down. You are done. You don't mind, you don't mind at all that there is still food left. You know you are not wasting food. The only way that you can waste food is to put food into your body when you are not even hungry. Then it goes to waste, it goes to your waist, and you don't need to waste food in that manner; you don't need it to go to your waist. Now, if there's quite a bit of food left over, you might put it in a container and save it for later, or throw it in the trash or the compost. You don't mind. You don't mind at all. For you know you are not wasting food. The only way that you can waste food is to put food into your body when you are not truly hungry and then it goes to waste, it goes to your waist, and you don't need it going to your waist. Now, if there's quite a bit of food left over you might put it in a container and save it for later, or throw it in the trash or the compost. You don't mind. You don't mind at all. For you know you are not wasting food. The only way that you can waste food is to put food into your body when you are not truly hungry and then it goes to waste, it goes to your waist, and you don't need it going to your waist. You don't mind, you don't mind at all that there is still food left on your plate, for you are not a child, you are not a child and no one can make you clean your plate. You are not a child and no one can make you clean your plate. You are an adult. You are not a child and no one can make you clean your plate. In fact you are an adult and you defy, you defy *anyone* to make you clean your plate. You defy *anyone* to make you clean your plate by always leaving food on your plate. Sometimes you leave half the plate of food, or even more depending on how you feel; other times it's just a few bites or so. You always leave food on your plate, just to show that you are the one who is in control, that you are defiant. Sometimes you leave half the plate of food or even more depending on how you feel; other times it's just a few bites or so. You always leave food on your plate, just to show that you are the one who is in control, that you are defiant. And it helps in another way as well because it helps you to avoid those full, stuffed, heavy, sluggish, slow, bloated and sloth-like sensations. You hate feeling bloated; you hate feeling uncomfortable. You'll do anything to avoid these awful feelings and sensations. On the other hand, there have been times when you were a bit on the empty side and it feels good. You know what I mean. There were times when you were a youngster and you are playing outside and it's near dinnertime and you're a bit on the empty side; but you don't mind, you don't mind at all. You're having way too much fun just playing and being active. You don't mind that you're a bit on the empty side. It feels good. You feel light, alive, energetic and enthusiastic. It feels good. Somewhere in the back of your mind is the hope, the desire, that your mother or someone will not be calling you in for dinner, because you're having way too much fun just playing and being active. You don't mind that you're a bit on the empty side. It feels good. You feel light, alive, energetic and enthusiastic. It feels good. And if your mother or someone does call you in for dinner, you pretend as though you never heard a thing. You ignore their calls because you're having way too much fun just playing and being active. You don't mind that you're a bit on the empty side. It feels good. You feel light, alive, energetic and enthusiastic. It feels good.

If your mother or someone is finally successful at getting you to come in for dinner, you just do the obligatory. You eat a few bites of this and that, just to satisfy them, so that you can excuse yourself from the table and get right back out to playing and being active. As you leave the table you don't mind at all that you are still a bit on the empty side. You don't mind at all because you feel light, alive, energetic and enthusiastic. It feels good. It feels so much better than those full, stuffed, heavy, sluggish, slow, bloated and sloth-like sensations that you despise. You would rather feel light, alive, energetic and enthusiastic. It feels good.

Metabolism

Metabolism is a script I use a lot. I usually like to use this during a client's second session. This script is fairly lengthy so you will want to familiarize yourself with it beforehand.

It is necessary to educate your client about metabolism and this piece prior to beginning the patter. During the intake portion of the client's first session, I ask how he or she feels about their metabolism. Usually the client will say something like it's slow, or non-existent, or they just don't know. If you know a lot about metabolism, you can develop your own talk or you can use the following information to educate your client.

As we mature, our metabolism tends to slow. A short article that I had read recently said that when a man turns 40 he can expect to gain a pound or so a year just based on slowing metabolism. At first that might not seem like much, but, as we continue to live, it begins to add up. Women are probably less fortunate. There are certain milestones in a woman's biology that tend to take a bigger hit on the metabolism.

Probably the main thing that determines our metabolism is muscle to fat ratio. If we have a good muscle to fat ratio, then the metabolism tends to hold—even in those times when we might miss out on our regular exercise or diet routines. Perhaps we're out of town, or ill, or maybe we have guests visiting. These things tend to break up our normal routines. When we have a good muscle to fat ratio, the metabolism tends to hold. Once we get flipped over and no longer have a good muscle to fat ratio, we may find ourselves in a constant struggle.

Obviously, exercise is an important element for keeping the metabolism working in our favor. A good thing to know is that for each additional pound of muscle that we add to our bodies, it takes another fifty calories a day to support that additional muscle mass. So it's easy to see that we can have a positive effect on the metabolism through exercise.

It's important to let your clients know ahead of time that this is a very visual process, and most people do well with the visual process. However, if your client finds that he or she doesn't readily get visual images, then just have the client convert the words into whatever works best. Feel, sense, experience: Make sure the client knows that the things I say are happening just as I say they are. This is especially important when doing groups.

It's also important for the client to maintain some contact with the hypnotist. It's important that the client has a conscious memory of the process so that he or she can perform it independently whenever desired. You can tell your client ahead of time that you may ask them something like, "Are you aware of the sound of my voice?" If the client hears that, then he or she can just nod or in some way let the hypnotist know that there is still a connection. This can make it easier for the hypnotist to know where the client is in trance. If the client doesn't readily respond, become more insistent. If there is still no response, you can use his or her name, which usually makes the client more aware.

Let the client know that you will be asking him or her to imagine some things going on in the body. Intellectually, we know these things are not going on in the body. However, the subconscious mind works in metaphor and the subconscious mind converts these images into the process that we need.

I refer to the example of Dr. O. Carl Simonton, who uses images of Pac Men running around in the body gobbling up cancer cells. We know that there are no Pac Men running around in our bodies gobbling up cancer cells, but the subconscious converts these images into the healing that we need. Tell the client that that's what we will be doing today. We won't have Pac Men running around gobbling up fat cells (although that is imagery that might work for some people). We will, however, be imagining some things that may seem pretty ridiculous. The subconscious mind tends to hang on to these ridiculous images even more so. While there are hypnotists who have written protocols for this sort of thing that are very scientific and describe the inner workings very accurately, they are probably doing it for their own intellectual minds. Our subconscious minds could care less. Images of Donald Duck or Bugs Bunny running around might be more effective.

You might want to use the Stairs for Metabolism as part of your induction (see following section). When you read it, you will first probably notice how it helps to set the stage for the Metabolism script. I usually follow the Metabolism script with the Hot Beach script. In the client's (or group's) following session, I will use the Metabolism II script just to keep things moving in the right direction, followed by the Hot Beach script again.

The Stairs for Metabolism Script

Ten—Feel yourself beginning to move down the stairs.

Nine—Feel yourself going deeper and deeper.

Eight—Moving further down the stairs, closer to that special place; your special place of comfort, relaxation and safety; that special place where today we are *cranking up the metabolism.* Yes, we're *speeeeeeeeding up the metabolism,* so that each bite of food, each calorie, each gram of fat, each bit of carbohydrate that enters into your system is burned up thoroughly and completely and converted into heat and energy for the body. As a result, you're more alive, energetic and enthusiastic. The pounds melt away like butter on a hot summer's day.

Seven—Going deeper and deeper and deeper down, feeling more relaxed even than before.

Six—Going deeper and deeper inside.

Five—Moving further down the stairs, closer to that special place; your special place of comfort, relaxation and safety; that special place where today we are *cranking up the metabolism.* Yes, we're *speeeeeeeeding up the metabolism,* so that each bite of food, each calorie, each gram of fat, each bit of carbohydrate that enters into your system is burned up thoroughly and completely and converted into heat and energy for the body. As a result, you're more alive, energetic and enthusiastic. The pounds melt away like butter on a hot summer's day.

Four—Moving further down the stairs, going deeper and deeper down.

Three—Going deeper and deeper inside.

Two—Almost down the stairs now, almost to that special place; your special place of comfort, relaxation and safety; that special place where today we are *cranking up the metabolism.* Yes, we're *speeeeeeeeding up the metabolism,* so that each bite of food, each calorie, each gram of fat, each bit of carbohydrate that enters into your system is burned up thoroughly and completely and converted into heat and energy for the body. As a result, you're more alive, energetic and enthusiastic. The pounds melt away like butter on a hot summer's day.

One—All the way down the stairs now, all the way to that special place; your special place of comfort, relaxation and safety; that special place that is just right for you.

Notice that door or gate. Notice how big it is. Notice what shape it is. Notice what it's made of. Is it iron, is it wood, or is it some other material? Now reach out and touch that door or gate. Notice how it feels. Is it rough, or is it smooth? Is it warm, or is it cool? Now push open that door or gate and walk through into your special place, your special place of comfort, safety and relaxation.

Notice what you see or feel. Notice the temperature of the air on your skin. Notice what kind of day it is. Is the sun shining? Is the sky blue? Are there clouds?

Notice any sounds. Perhaps there are the sounds of water, or a gentle breeze, or some other comforting sounds. Perhaps it's just the peace and quiet.

Notice any smells. This is your special place and it's just right for you. And you can come here anytime you want, any time at all, to just relax, to be creative, or to solve some problem. It's your special place and it's just right for you. Now take a deep breath and breathe in all of these good feelings and sensations. Breathe them in to every cell of your body.

The Metabolism Script

Experience yourself looking at yourself. Experience yourself looking at yourself, and you are going to begin by focusing on the area from your waist up. To be more specific, you are going to start by focusing on the area of your head. And to be even more specific than that, you are going to begin by focusing in on the area of your mouth and jaw. As you focus in on the area of your own mouth and jaw, it's just like looking through an X-ray. And, just like looking through an X-ray, you can see all of the inner workings of the mouth and jaw area. You can see the jawbones, the jaw muscles, the teeth, the tongue, and all of the interrelated parts—just like looking through an X-ray. Now, experience yourself putting a bite of food into your mouth and, just like in an X-ray, you can see the bite of food entering your mouth. Soon you begin to chew the bite of food. And, just like in an X-ray, you can see the teeth chewing and grinding away at the bite of food. And, just like in an X-ray, you can see the jawbones moving up and down and the jaw muscles expanding and contracting, the tongue pushing the bite of food this way and that for maximum efficiency. You notice you take your time; you take a good, long time, and chew each bite of food slowly and completely. For as you know, the mouth, the teeth are the first part of the digestive system and it's important that you chew each bite slowly and completely. You notice that when you chew each bite slowly and completely you gain a great deal more satisfaction from each bite. Yes, because you chew each bite slowly and completely, you gain much more enjoyment from each bite of food and you feel more easily satisfied. You notice you stop eating sooner because you feel more satisfied.

Now experience yourself swallowing that bite of food and, just like in an X-ray, you can see the bite of food moving down the esophagus. As the bite of food moves further and further down the esophagus it gets closer and closer to the stomach, and as it gets closer and closer to the stomach you begin to notice something. You begin to notice that it is like there's a furnace in the stomach, and there's a fire in the furnace in the stomach. As the bite of food reaches the end of the esophagus it drops into the furnace in the stomach and into the flames of the fire in the furnace in the stomach. The bite of food becomes fuel for the flames of the fire in the furnace in the stomach. You begin to notice something else. You notice that the flames of the fire in the furnace in the stomach are not all that great. And you begin to notice something else and that is that there is a dial on the side of the furnace in the stomach. You notice that the dial is marked from low to high. And you notice that the dial is set more toward the low side. So just experience yourself beginning to turn that dial up. As you turn that dial up, the flames begin to grow. The flames get larger and larger and more air is introduced into the furnace and the flames get hotter and hotter and larger and larger. Keep turning that dial up until the flames begin to *roar* and you can feel the heat pouring off the flames of the fire in the furnace in the stomach. Now each bite of food that drops into the flames of the fire in the furnace in the stomach is burned up completely and converted into heat and energy for the body. Each calorie, each gram of fat, each bit of carbohydrate is burned up thoroughly and completely and converted into heat and energy for the body. Every bite of food, every calorie, each gram of fat, every bit of carbohydrate is burned up thoroughly and completely and converted into heat and energy for your body. Yes, that's right, every bite of food, every calorie, every gram of fat, every bit of carbohydrate is burned up thoroughly and completely and converted into heat and energy for the body. You begin to notice something else. You begin to notice that there is plumbing running through the furnace in the stomach. This plumbing is the circulatory system. The blood flows through the plumbing in the furnace in the stomach to pick up heat and energy for the body. The blood flowing through the plumbing is becoming super-heated and super-energized, which means we need to compensate for that; it means we need to speed up the flow of the circulatory system; and that means we need to speed up the pumping mechanism, *the heart.* Just bring your attention to the area of your own heart and imagine a large pumping mechanism working away. It could be one of those old steam driven pumps that just seems to run on and on forever; or it could be an oil field pump that runs day after day, year after year, on and on endlessly. Or it could be any type of pumping mechanism that you might imagine. Notice that there is a dial on the side of the pumping mechanism. This dial on the side of the pump is marked from low to high. Once again, you need to turn the dial up, but just a little bit this time, just enough to increase the flow slightly. So begin to turn that dial up until the pump starts pumping a bit faster—that's right, right about there. Now see, feel, experience, notice that pumping mechanism running just a bit more quickly. And see, feel, notice the blood flowing through the circulatory system just a bit more quickly. Now there are lots of different kinds of pumps, but all pumps work in one of two ways. Some pumps pump a lot of pressure, like the pump you would use to pump up your car tire. That pump pumps a lot of pressure. Other pumps don't pump much pressure; they work by drawing fluid through a line, much like you would suck water through a straw. And that's the kind of pumping mechanism you have here. Even though you've increased the flow, the pressure in the lines remains the same. It's just moving through the lines more quickly.

If you are someone who has experienced an imbalance in the pressure in your lines, there is a valve on the pump (much like a faucet for the hose on the side of a house) with a gauge. If you want to turn the pressure in the lines down, turn the valve in a clockwise manner. If you want to turn the pressure up, turn the valve in a counterclockwise manner. Watch the gauge until the pressure is right where you desire. It doesn't take much to adjust the pressure to where you desire.

As the blood flows through the plumbing in the furnace in the stomach, it picks up the heat and energy from the fire in the furnace in the stomach and it begins to carry this super-warmed, super-energized blood throughout the body. This super-warmed, super-energized blood is also a super-healing blood. As the blood flows, it flows into the internal organs creating a super-warm, super-energized, tingling sensation, rinsing away any toxins, any unwanted particles, any discolorations, any discomfort, any disease; rinsing it away and flushing it away, out through the body's natural filtration system.

As the blood begins to flow towards the extremities, it flows up into the neck and throat and into the cranial area, again rinsing away any toxins, any unwanted particles, any discomforts, any disease, all throughout the cranial area, leaving behind a super-warm, super-healing and tingling sensation throughout the cranial area, right to the very cells of the scalp.

As the blood flows toward the outer extremities, it begins flowing through the shoulders and out into the arms. You can just feel the warm healing fluid moving through your shoulder muscles and shoulder joints, rinsing away any toxins, any unwanted particles, any impurities, any discomforts, any disease; rinsing them away, flushing them away, leaving behind a super-warming, super-energized, healing, tingling sensation. As the blood flows down through the arms, the elbows, it's rinsing away any toxins, any unwanted particles, any discolorations, any discomforts, any disease; rinsing them away, to be flushed out through the body's natural filtration system. As the blood flows into the hands and fingers, you can feel the super-warm fluid flowing into your hands and the very tips of your fingers, leaving behind a super-healing, super-warm, energized, tingling sensation. Feel that super-warm fluid filling your hands and fingers.

As the blood flows down to the lower extremities, it flows down through the hips and into the thighs. Feel that warm healing fluid flowing through your hip muscles and your hip joints, rinsing away any toxins, any unwanted particles, any impurities, any discomforts, any disease, leaving behind a super-warm, super-energized, super-healing, tingling sensation. Feel the warm healing fluid flowing down through your thighs and flowing into the knees, cleansing and healing and energizing, flowing down into the calves and shins and down through the ankles, leaving behind a super-warm, super-energized, tingling sensation.

As the blood flows into the feet and toes, feel the warm fluid flowing into your feet and toes. Notice the super-warm, super-healing, tingling sensation. Feel that super-warm fluid flowing into your feet and toes. Notice how warm and tingly your feet and toes now feel, as if you had your feet in one of those super-warm bath machines—the kind that you put your feet into the hot water and Epsom salts, and it vibrates and massages your feet in the hot water and Epsom salts. It feels so good and it's coming from the inside. Notice that super-warm, super-energized, healing, tingling sensation all throughout your entire body.

Now, something else has happened. Because we have sped up the metabolism, because we have increased the flames of the fire in the furnace in the stomach, something else has occurred. We have created a greater demand for fuel. That fuel needs to come from fuel that's been stored throughout the body in the form of fat cells. This is the job of the circulatory system as well. The blood cells flow throughout the body and pick up fat cells and carry them back to the furnace in the stomach to deposit them into the flames of the fire in the furnace in the stomach. Just experience the blood cells picking up the fat cells and carrying them back through the plumbing in the furnace in the stomach and depositing them right into the flames of the fire in the furnace in the stomach. As each fat cell drops into the flames of the fire in the furnace in the stomach, the flames *leap and crack and snap and pop with delight. You can feel the bursts of heat and energy blasting off the flames of the furnace in the stomach.* As each fat cell drops into the flames of the fire in the furnace in the stomach, the flames *leap and crack and snap and pop with delight. You can feel the bursts of heat and energy blasting off the flames of the furnace in the stomach.* There may be some areas of your body where more fat cells are stored than others, and you can just experience the blood flowing to these areas and carrying fat cells back to the flames of the fire in the furnace in the stomach. Yes, as each blood cell passes through the plumbing in the furnace in the stomach, it deposits a fat cell directly into the flames of the fire in the furnace in the stomach. As each fat cell drops into the flames of the fire in the furnace in the stomach, the flames *leap and crack and snap and pop with delight. You can feel the bursts of heat and energy blasting off the flames of the furnace in the stomach.* With every beat of your heart, with every breath you take, fat cells are being carried away to the fire in the furnace in the stomach. With every beat of your heart, with every breath you take, you're becoming slimmer, trimmer, fitter and healthier.

It's nice to know that you are in control of these dials and you can turn them up or down any time you wish, and I encourage you to do so from time to time. And it's nice to know that your body is working more efficiently, more effectively than ever. Right this very moment you're very relaxed. Even though you are very relaxed right this very moment, your body is working more effectively, more efficiently than before. When you get up at the end of this session, you will weigh less than you did when you sat down, all because your body is working more efficiently, more effectively than ever before.

And it's nice to know that no matter where you are, no matter what you are doing, your body is working more efficiently, more effectively than ever before. When you are working, performing your normal tasks, *somewhere in the back of your mind there is this gnawing, this nagging, sensation that your body is working more efficiently, more effectively, than ever before.* You can feel the pounds slipping, sliding, dripping, dropping right off your body. You feel yourself as lighter, leaner, healthier. You move more freely, more easily, more gracefully. You notice your clothing fits you differently; perhaps you're wearing different kinds of clothing altogether. You feel better about yourself and who you are—more confident. Others treat you differently, making positive comments about your lean, healthy appearance.

Perhaps you are doing other normal kinds of things like shopping, and there are lots of different kinds of shopping we can do. Perhaps you find yourself going to the shopping mall from time to time. Around the holidays, just about everyone ends up at the shopping mall sooner or later. It's amazing how much exercise we get at the shopping mall. At a shopping mall, you might be going from this store to that store, hauling packages wherever you go, picking up this or that item, checking for bargains at this store or that store, comparing an item from this store to an item at that store, running here and there trying to get ideas for this person or that person. And, actually, you are getting a lot more exercise than you might be aware of. And the whole time in the back of your mind you have this awareness—this gnawing, nagging sensation—that your body is working more efficiently, more effectively than ever before.

There are other kinds of shopping that you might do as well, like at the grocery store. There you are at the grocery store pushing your cart down the aisle and you have this certain awareness in the back of your mind—a knowing, a gnawing, a nagging sensation—that your body is working more efficiently, more effectively than ever before, which only causes you to be more conscientious and to make the smarter, healthier choices that put you in control. You know certain nutrients, certain fuels, burn more efficiently in your body. You know your metabolism is working more efficiently for you and you want to keep it that way. You buy and use only the best nutrients, the best fuels for your body, to keep your body running at its best. As you approach the checkout counter, you begin to notice the tabloids; yes, you notice the tabloids; and as you notice the tabloids, *somewhere in the back of your mind there's a knowing—a gnawing, a nagging sensation—that your body is working more efficiently, more effectively than ever before.* You can feel the pounds slipping, sliding, dripping, dropping, falling right off your body. You feel yourself as lighter, leaner, healthier and fitter. You move more freely, more quickly, more easily and more gracefully. You notice your clothing fits you differently; perhaps you're wearing different kinds of clothing altogether. You feel better about yourself and who you are—more confident. Others treat you differently, making positive comments about your lean, healthy appearance.

When you exercise, when you exercise, your body is working eight times more effectively, eight times more effectively than ever before. That means that you are burning off eight times the calories, eight times the fat cells. Now, I'm not talking about some little namby pamby exercise. I'm talking about real exercise with real effort and real intention behind it. Your body is working eight times more effectively than before, which only encourages you to do even more. Perhaps you do more repetitions, or use more resistance, or keep at it longer, or with more effort, because your body is working eight times more effectively than ever before.

When you're sleeping, you sleep comfortably through, especially because you know your body is working more efficiently, more effectively than ever before. Even while you sleep, *somewhere in the back of your mind there is this knowing—this gnawing, this nagging sensation—that your body is working more efficiently, more effectively than ever before,* and you can feel the pounds slipping, sliding, dripping, dropping, falling right off your body. You feel yourself as lighter, leaner, healthier and fitter than ever before. You have good positive dreams that help to guide you through life. A lot of these good positive dreams are about your lean, healthy, fit body and wearing the kinds of clothes you want to wear. You wake up in the morning feeling alive, alert and refreshed and all of the time that you are sleeping, your body is working more efficiently, more effectively than before. While you're asleep your body is burning fat and calories and you get up in the morning weighing less than you did when you went to bed. And no matter where you are, no matter what you might be doing, *somewhere in the back of your mind there is this knowing—this gnawing, this nagging sensation—that your body is working more efficiently, more effectively than ever before,* and you can feel the pounds slipping, sliding, dripping, dropping right off your body. You feel yourself as lighter, leaner, healthier and fitter. The pounds are just melting away like butter on a hot summer day.

THE METABOLISM II SCRIPT

You might recall the last time we were together. We did some work on your metabolism. You might recall that furnace in your stomach. Just bring your attention to your stomach and that furnace in your stomach. This time it's a bit of a different furnace. This time it's a boiler furnace.

I would guess that we've all seen a movie at sometime with a steamship. Down in the bowels of that steamship is the boiler furnace room. Men are working busily down there in that boiler furnace room, shoveling scoop after scoop of coal through that boiler furnace door, heating up water to make steam for those big old steam engines. That's what's happening in your stomach right this very moment. Although it's not coal that these men are shoveling through the boiler furnace door, it's fat cells. Yes, these men are working, busily shoveling scoop after scoop of fat cells through that boiler furnace door. It's as if they are mining these fat cells from throughout your body, scoop after scoop of fat cells through that boiler furnace door. Each time they shovel a scoop full of fat cells through that boiler furnace door, the flames come licking back out at them. Their bodies glisten with sweat as they work so feverishly hard in the unbearable heat. Yet they continue shoveling scoop after scoop of fat cells through that boiler furnace door.

With each scoop of fat cells the boiler furnace is getting hotter and hotter. The heat begins to radiate throughout your body. You can feel it radiate up through your neck and throat into your cranial area. You can feel it radiate out through your shoulders, down through your arms, and into your hands and the very tips of your fingers. Feel it radiating down into your lower extremities. Feel it radiating down through your hips into your thighs, through your knees and calves and shins. Feel the heat radiating down into your feet and into your toes.

Notice the warm sensations throughout your body. How good it feels— so warm, so energizing. And somewhere in the back of your mind, there's a knowing, a gnawing sensation that your body's working more efficiently, more effectively than ever before. The pounds are dripping, dropping, falling, melting off of your body like butter on a hot summer's day.

The Hot Beach 7

When working with weight clients, it's important that they are able to create a good mental image of themselves at their ideal body size. Most people can do that easily. For people who did like their body size at some point, then take them to that point of reference and anchor those images. The hot beach is helpful for anyone to create the images of their lean healthy body. The hot beach is also good for those who have trouble creating images (maybe they were never lean). I usually follow the Metabolism script with the Hot Beach, and again later when I do the Metabolism Follow-Up.

The Hot Beach Script

Experience yourself standing on a hot sunny beach. The sun is just beating down upon you and it feels really good. You know how good it can feel to feel the hot sunrays penetrating your skin. It feels so good.

The sun is so hot that it heats up the sand beneath you to such an extent that the sand is reflecting the heat right back at you. It's as if you get a double effect, almost like being in an oven. It feels good to just stand on the hot sunny beach and bake in the hot sunshine.

Soon perspiration begins to form. It begins to form beads and the beads begin to form droplets and the droplets begin to form drops. The drops begin to drip, drip from your body. With each drop of perspiration, away drips toxins. Away drips calories. Away drips fat. Drip, drip, dripping away, melting away like butter on a hot summer's day. Yes, with each drop of perspiration, away drips toxins. Away drips calories. Away drips fat. Drip, drip, dripping away, melting away, like butter on a hot summer's day.

With each drop of perspiration, your body is becoming leaner and leaner and healthier. You can see, feel, imagine, notice, your body becoming leaner and leaner as each drop of perspiration drips away.

As you reach that body size that is just right for you, a cool breeze comes along and solidifies you right in that body size. Whenever you think of yourself, this is the way you think of yourself. A lean, healthy, fit individual.

Notice how your clothing fits your body. Perhaps you're wearing different clothing altogether. Notice how you move more easily, more freely, more quickly, more gracefully. You feel better about yourself and who you are—more confident. Others treat you differently, making positive comments about your lean, healthy, fit appearance.

Whenever you think of yourself, these are the kinds of thoughts and images you maintain. These good, healthy, thoughts and images of your lean, healthy, fit body. Any competing thoughts or images you banish from your mind. You replace them with these good healthy thoughts and images of your lean, healthy, fit body. For this is who you truly are. You are the kind of person who wears the kinds of clothing that you want to wear. Someone who moves easily and freely and gracefully—that's you. Someone who feels good about themself and who they are—that's you. Someone who others look to as a positive example—that's you. It feels good to think of yourself as a lean healthy individual.

Slim Feels

"Nothing tastes as good as slim feels." This is a catch phrase that has been used a lot in the weight industry. I was first aware of hearing it with Weight Watchers and, now, Jenny Craig. I use the phrase in my tapes and during my sessions, as well as in the following script. Shorten or lengthen the script (read over and over) according to the available time. I normally end weight sessions with this wording.

THE SLIM FEELS SCRIPT

Nothing tastes as good as slim feels. Nothing tastes as good as slim feels. Nothing tastes as good as slim feels. And slim and fit and trim and healthy feels wonderful. Slim and fit and trim and healthy feels fantastic. Slim and fit and healthy feels amazing *all the time.* Something only tastes on the lips for a few brief moments and it's gone. But slim and fit and healthy feels fantastic *all the time:* every second of every minute, every minute of every hour, every hour of every day, every day of every week, every week of every month, month after month, year after year. Slim and trim and fit and healthy feels fantastic, all the time.

Nothing tastes as good as slim feels. Nothing tastes as good as slim feels. Nothing tastes as good as slim feels. And slim and fit and trim and healthy feels wonderful. Slim and fit and trim and healthy feels fantastic. Slim and fit and healthy feels amazing *all the time.* Something only tastes on the lips for a few brief moments and it's gone. But slim and fit and healthy feels fantastic *all the time:* every second of every minute, every minute of every hour, every hour of every day, every day of every week, every week of every month, month after month, year after year. Slim and trim and fit and healthy feels fantastic, all the time.

Nothing tastes as good as slim feels. Nothing tastes as good as slim feels. Nothing tastes as good as slim feels. And slim and fit and trim and healthy feels wonderful. Slim and fit and trim and healthy feels fantastic. Slim and fit and healthy feels amazing *all the time.* Something only tastes on the lips for a few brief moments and it's gone. But slim and fit and healthy feels fantastic *all the time:* every second of every minute, every minute of every hour, every hour of every day, every day of every week, every week of every month, month after month, year after year. Slim and trim and fit and healthy feels fantastic, all the time.

Nothing tastes as good as slim feels. Nothing tastes as good as slim feels. Nothing tastes as good as slim feels.

Sodas

Too many people are drinking too much soda. Getting your calories from what you drink is not a good idea. There is no food value, just calories and chemicals. Some people say, "I only drink diet soda." I'm sorry to say that the news is not so good for diet sodas either. Even though there may be few if any calories in that diet soda, it keeps us craving something sweet. Research shows that people who drink diet sodas crave more food. The truth is we just don't need sodas.

I often follow this script with the water script (especially with groups), because they often go hand in hand.

THE SODAS SCRIPT

There is something about sodas. And when I talk about sodas, I'm talking about regular sodas and diet sodas, or other kinds of sweetened drinks like Kool Aid or Slurpies or Slushies, or sweetened teas or even sweetened coffee drinks. I'm not at all referring to natural fruit juices. I'm talking more about the more processed kinds of sweet drinks, such as regular sodas or diet sodas, and other kinds of sweetened drinks like Kool Aide or Slurpies or Slushies, and even sweetened teas or sweetened coffee drinks. These sweetened drinks all have one thing in common and that is that none of them live up to what it is that they are supposed to do. That is, none of them are really thirst quenching or refreshing or satisfying. You know what I mean.

For, what happens is, the moment that sweet drink begins to enter into your mouth, it puts an obnoxious, sticky, sweet coating on your tongue and throughout the inside of your mouth. You know what I mean. As soon as that sweetened drink enters into your mouth, it puts an obnoxious, sticky, sweet coating on your tongue and throughout the inside of your mouth. Nothing will penetrate this obnoxious, sticky, sweet coating over your tongue and throughout the inside of your mouth. You can drink and drink that sweetened drink; however, you will never feel refreshed or satisfied or have your thirst quenched. All you are doing is dumping unwanted calories and preservatives into your body and you never will feel satisfied.

Only cool, clear, refreshing water will satisfy your thirst. You begin drinking some cool, clear, refreshing water and, as you do, it flows over your tongue and throughout the inside of your mouth, quickly rinsing away that obnoxious, sticky, sweet coating. It feels good to feel the cool, clear, refreshing water flowing over your tongue and throughout the inside of your mouth. It feels so refreshing, so satisfying, so thirst quenching. Only cool, clear, refreshing water satisfies you. It feels good to drink cool, clear, refreshing water.

Water 10

As you are probably aware, drinking water is a good thing. Doctors and health professionals are constantly encouraging us to drink more water. Many of us simply don't drink enough water. Perhaps we got into the habit of drinking sodas, or other sweetened or alcoholic beverages. These kinds of drinks are not a good substitute for clean refreshing water.

Clients often comment that they are not drinking enough water and need to drink more. If we are trying to lose weight and are not drinking enough water, our bodies will seek out that moisture wherever possible. This means that our bodies will pull the moisture from the food that we ingest, and when that happens we pull more of the calories and fat in along with it.

If you ever notice yourself getting headaches after your workout, then you're probably not well hydrated. When you have clients who need to drink more water or have been using sweetened drinks instead of water, then the Water script and the Sodas script are great. I use these scripts in groups a lot. Watch people head for the water cooler after their session.

THE WATER SCRIPT

There was a time when you were a youngster and you are playing out-doors at recess time and it's a hot day. Perhaps you're involved in some organized event like a ball game; or perhaps it's something more loosely organized like jumping rope or hopscotch, or playing on the jungle gym or teeter totter, or swinging on the swings; or maybe you're playing some running game like tag. It's a hot day and you know as youngsters how we become all involved in what we are doing and become oblivious to our own surroundings and even our own body functions.

Then something happens to summon you back to the schoolhouse. Perhaps the bell rings or a teacher blows a whistle or yells or in some other way summons everyone back to the schoolhouse. As you head back to the schoolhouse you begin to realize just how hot and dry and thirsty and parched you have become. You can feel the hot, dry, thirsty, parched sensations in your mouth. As you notice the hot, dry, sensa-tions you begin thinking about the drinking fountain in the hallway. You pick up the pace and hurry back to the schoolhouse so that you can get to that drinking fountain in the hallway.

As you arrive at the drinking fountain in the hallway, you realize you are not the first one to have this idea. Yes, other youngsters have already lined up behind the drinking fountain in the hallway and you find your place at the end of the line. You're a bit anxious, because you don't know if there will be enough time for you to get a turn at the drinking fountain. Other youngsters are anxious as well and some of them are saying things to the person at the front of the line like, "Hurry up, we want a turn too," or, "Don't drink all of the water; save some for us." Perhaps someone gives that youngster at the front of the line a nudge of encouragement.

The longer you wait, the more certain you become that you will never get a turn at the drinking fountain. But it does become your turn and you grasp that cold faucet handle and you crank that water up. You begin sucking down that cool, clear, refreshing water as it hits your lips. You can feel that cool, clear, refreshing water flowing over your tongue and throughout the inside of your mouth. It feels so refreshing, so satisfying, so thirst quenching. It feels good to suck down gulp after gulp of cool, clear, clean, refreshing water. As you're sucking down gulp after gulp of cool, clear, clean, refreshing water, you're dreaming about being able to just stay at that drinking fountain forever and just suck down gulp after gulp of cool, clear, refreshing water, on and on forever.

Other youngsters are becoming anxious. They are saying things like, "Hurry up, we want a turn too," or, "Don't drink all of the water; we want some too." Perhaps someone from behind you gives you a nudge of encouragement; but you ignore their encouragements and continue sucking down gulp after gulp of cool, clear, clean, refreshing water. You continue dreaming about staying at that drinking fountain forever, and sucking down cool, clear, clean, refreshing water, on and on endlessly. It feels good to feel the cool, clear, refreshing water flowing over your tongue and throughout the inside of your mouth. It feels so refreshing, so satisfying, so thirst quenching. Nothing satisfies you like cool, clear, clean, refreshing water.

Then something happens to interrupt. The teacher is calling everyone back into the classroom. "It's time to clear the hall now. Everyone get back into the classroom." Even as you drag yourself away from that drinking fountain, you manage to get in those last few gulps of cool, clear, clean, refreshing water. As you walk back to the classroom you can feel the water sloshing around in your stomach. Back at your seat, you find yourself still dreaming about being at that water fountain forever and ever, sucking down cool, clear, refreshing water. It feels so good to feel the cool, clear, refreshing water flowing over your tongue and throughout the inside of your mouth. It feels so refreshing, so satisfying, so thirst quenching. Nothing satisfies you like cool, clear, refreshing water.

Pacing Chain around Control

Hypnotists are usually familiar with pacing and leading as an effective method to gently coax the subconscious mind into taking suggestions. *Pacing statements* are statements that are irrefutable (hard for the conscious mind to argue with). *Leading statements* are the statements that contain the suggestion that the hypnotist wants the client to follow.

The rule of thumb is three pacing statements, followed by a leading statement. This is not set in stone; however, you must have at least two pacing statements. More than three will work also. Notice in the following example that the first three statements are pacing statements, followed by a leading statement:

> You might notice the sound of the ventilation system when it comes on. You might notice people moving about in the building. You might notice a phone ringing somewhere in the building. And as you do, any of these sounds will take you deeper into relaxation.

This statement is part of normal sounds patter to help take a client into trance. It's hard for the mind to argue that they might notice the ventilation system, or people moving, or a phone ringing somewhere, so it will easily accept those statements (the pacing statements). Because everything we said leading up to the leading statement was acceptable to the mind, then it just tends to accept the next statement as truth as well (*any of these sounds will take you deeper into relaxation*).

The control script is what I refer to as a pacing chain. A pacing chain is where I just use a lot of pacing statements and very few leading statements. By using lots of these highly irrefutable statements, you can lead the client very nicely along. This is what I like to call, *leading the mind down the merry path.*

Control is an elusive creature. If we feel out of control, then we want to get back in control. People who are controlling always seem to want more. The Control script is a nice way to help people become grounded again. It works well in groups also.

The Control script herein is followed by a Smoking script that uses the same basic Control script and adapts it to smoking. A Food script then follows. Smoking and food are certainly two areas where people frequently feel out of control. You might notice that this script can easily be adapted to many different uses.

I have italicized some of the more important places to emphasize (embedded suggestions).

The Pacing Chain around Control Script

[This script follows some pacing and leading or other suggestions.]

And, as a result, you feel more in control, and you are in control. And you are the kind of person who takes control in their life. I know this because you are listening to this [or because you came into my office today] and that's the sort of good, healthy, intelligent choice a person makes who takes control in their life. And more and more, every day in every way, those are the kinds of good, healthy, intelligent choices you find yourself making—those kinds of good, healthy, intelligent choices that put you in control. And who better to be in control of your life than you? Who knows your needs and wants better than you do?

Sometimes we get caught up in the daily business of being a good parent, or a good employee, or a good provider. Oftentimes we don't allow ourselves the time to just allow ourselves to reflect and ask, "What is it I really need out of life? What is it that will allow me to live life to the fullest, to feel fulfilled?" And, as a result, it becomes more and more apparent to you just what you do need and want out of life to feel more fulfilled, to live life to its fullest. Perhaps you find yourself taking some time out to just reflect, or perhaps it comes to you in the form of a dream, or perhaps it just becomes more apparent in your daily life. As a result, you find yourself setting good healthy boundaries. Yes, you set good healthy boundaries to get your needs met in a good healthy way. And, as a result of setting good healthy boundaries and getting your needs met in a good healthy way, you feel more in control. Not only do you feel more in control, you *are* in control. And who better to be in control of your life than you? When we are in control, we make good healthy choices—we gain freedom. No longer do we give away our control, no longer do we give away our choices. We gain freedom and when we are in control we feel more confident. We feel better about ourselves and who we are. And when we feel better about ourselves and who we are, good things just seem to happen. Perhaps you've noticed this before. Perhaps there have been times in your life when you felt confident and good about yourself and who you are, and good things just seemed to happen. It is a phenomenon that just occurs. There's no explaining it; it just happens that way.

And now, more and more, every day and in every way, you notice good things happening to you. More and more, you find yourself in the right place at the right time. More and more, you find those people and situations that you desire in your life, flowing into your life. More and more, good things just come to you. More and more, you notice the good things, the positive things. Every day good things, positive things, occur; and more and more, you find yourself focusing on the good things, the positive. Even on the worst day something good, something positive, occurs; and more and more, you find yourself focusing on the good, the positive. The more you notice the good, the positive, the more good positive things actually occur. It's a compounding effect. The more we notice it happening, the more it happens. More and more, you see the good, the positive, in every person and situation. More and more, you see the joy in life. More and more, you see the joy in your life. More and more, you notice the joy in every person and situation. As a result, for you the sun shines a little brighter. The sky is bluer. The grass is greener. The air is fresher. You walk with a new spring, a new bounce in your step. For you, stumbling blocks become stepping-stones. Yes, for you, stumbling blocks become stepping stones on the path of life, allowing you to see the path ahead more clearly, to move ahead more confidently, to move ahead more quickly; allowing you to see ahead into the future, knowing that good things are coming to you. Yes, things that were once problems you work through in a good healthy way; become strengths that you rely upon; strengths that allow you to move ahead into life with new confidence, a new boldness; taking on all that life has to offer with a new confidence, a new power. As a result, more and more, every day in every way, you feel better about yourself and who you are. You feel more alive, energetic and enthusiastic than the day before. The next time that you step outside into the air, and every time you step outside into the air, you notice a new energy, a new electricity, flowing through the air and into your body, causing you to feel alive, more energetic and enthusiastic. More and more, every day and in every way, you're better and better, looking forward to each new day and what it has to offer you.

SUGGESTIONS AROUND CONTROL SCRIPT (SMOKING)

[This script follows other suggestion work, or deepening, or pacing and leading.]

More and more, you are in control. Yes, and you are someone who takes control. I know this because you came here today and that is the sort of action a person takes who takes control in their life. It's the sort of good, healthy, intelligent choice a person makes who takes control in their life. More and more, those are the kinds of choices you find yourself making more and more—those kinds of good, healthy, intelligent decisions that put you in control. And who better to be in control of your life than you? Who knows your wants and needs better than you do? Certainly not some weed rolled up in a piece of paper. No! Some weed rolled up in a piece of paper has no business controlling your life. From now on you take control. You make the choices.

You set good healthy boundaries. Yes, you set good healthy boundaries to get your needs met in a good healthy way. As a result of setting good healthy boundaries and getting your needs met in a good healthy way, you *feel more in control.* Not only do you *feel more in control, you are in control.* And who better to be in control of your life than you? Certainly not some weed rolled up in a piece of paper. No! Some weed rolled up in a piece of paper has no business controlling your life. From now on you make the choices. You take control. You make the choices that give you freedom—the freedom to live your life in the good healthy manner that you choose, no longer allowing some weed rolled up in a piece of paper to steal away your freedom. No! You take control. You choose freedom—the freedom to live your healthy new lifestyle in a way that you desire.

And when you're in control, you *feel more confident;* and when you *feel more confident,* you *feel better about yourself and who you are;* and when you *feel better about yourself and who you are,* good things just seem to happen. Perhaps you've experienced this before. Perhaps there was a time in your life when you felt confident and felt good about yourself and good things just seemed to happen. There's no explaining it; it's just a phenomenon that occurs. More and more now, every day in every way, you find good things happening to you. More and more, you find yourself in the right place at the right time. More and more, you find those people and situations that you desire in your life, flowing into your life.

More and more, you focus on the positive, the good, the healthy, the beneficial. More and more, you see the positive, the good, in every person and situation. Every day, good things, positive things, occur; and more and more, you focus on the good, the positive, the healthy, the beneficial. Even on the worst day something good, something positive, occurs. More and more, you experience the good, the positive, the healthy, the beneficial, in every person and situation.

Your new in-control lifestyle is a more positive lifestyle. You experience more freedom, more options; more opportunities come your way.

Suggestions around Control Script (Food)

[This script follows other suggestion work or deepening.]

More and more, you are in control. Yes, and you are someone who takes control. I know this because you came here today and that is the sort of action a person takes who takes control in their life. It's the sort of good, healthy, intelligent choice a person makes who takes control in their life. More and more, those are the kinds of choices you find yourself making more and more—those kinds of good, healthy, intelligent decisions that put you in control. And who better to be in control of your life than you? Who knows your wants and needs better than you do? Certainly not food. No! Food has no business controlling your life. From now on you take control. You make the choices.

You set good healthy boundaries. Yes, you set good healthy boundaries to get your needs met in a good healthy way. As a result of setting good healthy boundaries and getting your needs met in a good healthy way, you feel more in control. Not only do you feel more in control, you are in control. And who better to be in control of your life than you? Certainly not food. No! Food has no business controlling your life. From now on you make the choices. You take control. You make the choices that give you freedom—the freedom to live your life in the good healthy manner that you choose. No longer do you allow food to steal away your freedom. No! You take control. You choose freedom—the freedom to live your healthy new lifestyle in a way that you desire.

And when you're in control, you *feel more confident;* and when you *feel more confident,* you *feel better about yourself and who you are;* and when you *feel better about yourself and who you are,* good things just seem to happen. Perhaps you've experienced this before. Perhaps there was a time in your life when you felt confident and felt good about yourself and good things just seemed to pop right into your life. There's no explaining it; it's just a phenomenon that occurs. More and more now, every day in every way, you find good things happening to you. More and more, you find yourself in the right place at the right time. More and more, you find those people and situations that you desire in your life, flowing into your life.

More and more, you focus on the positive, the good. More and more, you experience the positive, the good, in every person and situation. Every day, good things, positive things, occur; and more and more, you focus on the good, the positive, the healthy, the beneficial. Even on the worst day something good, something positive, occurs. More and more, you experience the good, the positive, the healthy, the beneficial in every person and situation.

Your in-control lifestyle is a positive lifestyle. You experience more freedom, more options; more opportunities come your way as a result.

Crossroads 12

The use of the Crossroads in hypnosis has been around for a long time and is a viable piece. I am giving you two Crossroads scripts here: One script is for use with weight and the other is for smoking. The smoking Crossroads is loosely based on Jerry Kein's version.

The Crossroads can be used for lots of different issues. It can help to motivate the client to get off the fence and make a decision about that career move or relationship. The Crossroads can also be done as an interactive process. The therapist asks the client in trance to describe what will happen on the left road if the client continues along in this undesirable way. Then, turning to the right road, what happens as the client moves down this road using a changed behavior (or whatever).

It's important to gain the most effect of the crossroads when you set it up. Basically, the client is at a fork in the road. One fork is the direction of the poor choice if he or she continues with the same behavior as before. How will that choice affect the client further down the road? I have had the Crossroads done on me a number of times and I've noticed that most hypnotists are not very conscious of how they set it up.

Make certain that you have the unwanted or negative behavior on the left fork of the road. Psychologically, we associate left as more negative, such as "out in left field," or "left out," or "left wing," or "leftist." Even if we might take pride in being left wing, it still has a negative connotation attached to it.

Put the positive or new wanted behavior on the right road. After all, this is the *right road.* So we are subtly telling the subconscious that this is the right way to go. Even in my script, it says that as you turn from that road (the left road), you turn to the right road—the road of good, healthy, intelligent choices (or whatever).

THE CROSSROADS SCRIPT
(WEIGHT)

Experience yourself standing at a fork in the road. As you look down the fork that leads to the left, you notice it's a cold, barren, unfriendly road. This is the road of poor unhealthy choices. Along this road there are lots of food choices, although it's difficult to refer to these things as food, since they have so little nutritional value. Along this road is an abundance of junk food, sweets, sodas, fattening foods, foods high in refined carbohydrates, and all that you could possibly want.

What's missing from this road is that there are no hiking and biking trails; there are no mountains to climb, no rivers or lakes or streams to swim or boat or recreate in. There are no gyms or playing courts. There are, however, lots of big overstuffed couches and chairs. There are lots of TVs and VCRs and remote controls.

There is lots of clothing, like athletic wear for instance; however, it's the big baggy sweats—none of the formfitting active wear. There is every-day clothing as well, but it's more like big muumuus and things. Business wear, again, is the more oversized loose fitting muumuus, certainly not the nicely tailored professional looking clothes. Eveningwear is again restricted to the big oversized choices, and there is the great big underwear as well.

This road, the road of poor unhealthy choices, also leads to illness and surgeries and a shortened life. There's time and opportunities that are missed with friends and family. There's an early death and time missed with children and grandchildren. It's a sad road.

As you turn from that road, you look down the right road. You see a beautiful road. The sun is shining brightly in a deep rich blue sky. The trees are full of leaves. The grass is green. The birds sing and the wildlife play in the fresh clean air. This is the road of good healthy choices. As you begin to walk down this road, you notice that there are all kinds of good healthy eating choices—lots of good, healthy, fresh fruits and vegetables growing right up out of Mother Earth, there for the picking. There are trees and bushes full of fruits and berries.

There are mountains to climb, rivers, lakes and streams to swim and boat and recreate in. There are lots of opportunities for exercise. There are gyms and tennis and racquetball and basketball courts and more.

There are lots of clothing options as well. There is athletic wear, the nice, formfitting kind that you would like to be seen in. There is everyday clothing like blue jeans and things, but, again, the more formfitting, form flattering kinds. Business wear is tailored and professional looking. With eveningwear there are lots and lots of options and, again, all the more tailored and formfitting kinds of things that you really want to wear.

This road, the road of good healthy choices, leads to a long happy life. It leads to opportunities and adventures. It leads to time to spend with friends and family, children, grandchildren and great-grandchildren.

Any time you make a choice about your lifestyle, whether it has to do with what you put in your mouth or the exercise that you do or don't get, then you are choosing one of these roads.

More and more, it feels good to choose the right road. The road of good healthy choices.

THE CROSSROADS SCRIPT
(SMOKING)

Experience yourself standing at a fork in the road. As you look down the road that leads to the left, you notice it's a cold, barren, unfriendly road—like an old black and white movie. The sky is dreary; a cold wind blows the mist and drizzle. The trees are barren of leaves. The grass has long been replaced by cold hard rock. This is the road of smoker. This road leads to pain, suffering and an early death. This is a sad road. It's cold, lifeless and dead.

As you turn from that road you look down the right road. You see a beautiful road. The sun is shining brightly in a deep rich blue sky. The trees are full of leaves. The grass is green. The birds sing and the wildlife play in the fresh clean air.

This is the road of a non-smoker. This road leads to a long, healthy, fit life. As you begin walking down this road, you feel a warm gentle breeze playing in your hair. With each step you feel healthier and healthier, stronger and fitter. As you walk further and further down this road, you know there is no way that anyone or anything could ever make you turn back to that cold unfriendly road of a smoker.

You choose life—the long healthy life of a non-smoker—for the rest of your life.

Body Parts 13

"I hate my butt." "I hate my thighs." "I hate my arms." You've probably heard people make these kinds of statements. Perhaps you've heard these kinds of words coming from your own mouth. It's easy to become frustrated when we are struggling with our weight. There seem to be certain areas of the body that tend to be more of an issue for people, and it varies from individual to individual.

As hypnotists, we are aware of the power of the subconscious and our imagination, as well as the power of the words and thoughts that we have. We use positive terminology in the suggestions that we give our clients. What's happening when we use negative thoughts and words in regard to our own bodies? What is happening is this: We are asking for the very thing that we don't want. If someone says, "I hate my fat thighs," they are working to create the very thing that they do not want. That person is saying over and over that they have fat thighs, which only serves to create what they don't want. Like the once popular comedian, Flip Wilson, used to say, "What you see is what you get."

Hate is not a healing emotion. What would you do without that body part that you keep cursing? Don't you really need those legs or stomach? Haven't those body parts really served you well in the past? What would happen if we turned that around and started focusing more positive energy toward those body parts? That's what the Body Parts script encourages. I use this script a lot when doing groups, as well as for individuals who may be dealing with this issue. I address the issue prior to trance, just like I did on this page.

THE BODY PARTS SCRIPT

Perhaps you have some part of your body that you've become discouraged with. You might find yourself saying things like, "I hate my thighs," or, "I hate my stomach," or, "I hate my butt." Hate is not a healing emotion. These kinds of words and thoughts have only served to reinforce what it is that we don't want.

It's time to turn all that negativity around. It's time to start thinking of your body in a more positive way.

Imagine yourself holding that body part, holding it in your arms in the same manner that you would gently hold a baby. If that body part is your arms, that's fine. Just hold your arms in that manner. Experience yourself gently rocking and soothing that body part.

Experience yourself asking forgiveness for what you may have said or thought about it in the past. Now promise the body part that from now on you're only going to think and speak about it in the most nurturing, loving, positive ways.

Bootstraps/ High Diving Board/ Goal

14

These three scripts are all motivational. They are designed to help someone pick themselves up and get moving or to inspire them to move ahead. Familiarize yourself with each of the scripts and choose the one that will best suit your client.

THE BOOTSTRAPS SCRIPT

There is something I've noticed while working with you. It's that you possess a certain quality, something that not everyone has. It's a certain kind of tenacity, a toughness. I'll bet there was a time in your life when the world seemed to be coming down around you, a time when there wasn't someone around who could pick you up and help put things back together for you. It was one of those times when you just had to rely on yourself to put things back together and make your life work. It's one of those moments that I refer to as *picking yourself up by the bootstraps* and pulling things together and making it work, no matter what. You may know exactly what I'm referring to. It's not easy, but you make it happen.

Once we've had one of those bootstrap experiences, it gives us some inner wisdom, some character. From then on, somewhere in the back of the mind, we know that there is nothing that life can throw at us that we can't take on fully. We gain a certain inner strength, an ability to plow ahead no matter what. Not everyone possesses that ability. From then on we move ahead a bit more easily, a bit more confidently.

Perhaps now is a time when you need to use some of that *grab yourself by the bootstraps* energy and just know that you're moving ahead now, no matter what.

THE HIGH DIVING BOARD SCRIPT

Perhaps you recall as a youngster the first time you ever went off the high diving board. Maybe you had watched other youngsters jumping off and wished that you could do it to. Probably you found yourself walking near the high board and looking, sizing it up. Others may have teased you or dared you to try it.

Maybe you found yourself climbing the ladder, only to become scared and climb back down, perhaps many times. When you did get to the top maybe you froze, or found it difficult to walk out on the board or look down. If someone else came up the board, you might have stepped aside or climbed back down. Maybe you even felt embarrassed at times. Maybe others prodded you on. Perhaps you eased your way out to the end of the board a number of times looking down at the water below, only to move back away.

At some point, you found yourself standing at the end of the board, stepping out into space, trusting that gravity will do what it's supposed to do, and that the water will be there to do its job as well. Once you've stepped out into space there's no turning back. Suddenly you hit the water, perhaps there's a bit of sting and you're shooting down, down, deeper and deeper. The light at the surface gets further and further away. A new kind of fear begins to come over you as you begin to scramble to the surface.

As you break the surface, you gasp for air and exhilaration comes over you. You scramble to the edge and pull yourself up out of the water, breathing heavily, your heart pounding. You smile from ear to ear. Perhaps others are congratulating you.

Soon you find yourself at the top of the high board once again and you jump off more quickly now. Soon you are scrambling out of the pool and back up to the top of the high board, over and over again. What once was fear that held you back is now excitement. It feels exhilarating now.

The Goal Script

I can tell that you are the kind of person who knows how to set a goal. You are the kind of person who, when you put your mind to something, you achieve it. You know how to set goals and achieve them. I'll bet you set goals in your business life [*could add some client specifics here, like maybe you know they have sales quotas, etc.*] or in other areas. Sometimes, we set goals for things and don't even realize that is what we are doing. Most of us completed school and got a diploma. Sure, it may have seemed as though we didn't have much of a choice, but I'll bet that everyone thought of themselves getting that diploma and moving on to the next stage in life.

When we decide to go to college or trade school or even join the military, we have something long range in mind. Perhaps there was a time when someone thinks, "Gee, it might be nice to own my own home." As time goes on, what seemed to be a passing thought begins to make more and more sense. We might find ourselves dreaming about what kind of home we could afford, or what kind of neighborhood we might like to live in. Perhaps we begin putting away money for a down payment. We might find ourselves driving through potential neighborhoods. At some point, we might talk to a real estate agent or a mortgage lender. One day we find ourselves at a closing table receiving papers of ownership.

Maybe there was a time when you saw a place on TV, or in a magazine, or in the movies, and you thought something like, "Wouldn't it be nice to visit there?" As time goes by, that idea begins to take shape. Maybe you started looking at travel brochures and travel expenses. Maybe you started saving money and planning your schedule, until one day you find yourself in some exciting new place—all because you had some seemingly fleeting thought that developed into a goal that you achieved. The point is that most of us can and do set goals, even if we're not always aware that we are.

Sometimes we find it easy, even normal, to set goals for work or family. It can become normal to focus on those things and lose focus on ourselves and what we need. We don't often use our own abilities to achieve goals to just get our own needs met. It's easy, it seems, to put our own needs on the back burner. If we don't make ourselves a priority, where will we end up? Achieving all of those other things won't be possible if we're no longer around to make them happen.

We need to give ourselves the same sort of importance that we would to that next business project or community service, or whatever. What if you were to set goals for yourself and pursue them with the same tenacity that you pursue a project at work? What about that [workout routine/healthy eating/writing a book, *etc., etc.*] that has not been a priority?

More and more, doesn't it make sense to take better care of yourself?

Barnyard Fun 15

Barnyard fun is an aversion script. I don't normally use aversion methods as my first line of defense. Some hypnotists say they will never use them; however, aversion methods can be very effective and I will use anything that will get my clients to their goal.

Barnyard fun is a script I use on clients who have seen me previously for smoking, and then down the road they returned when something happened and they started smoking again. Usually it's because some stressful situation occurred or maybe they just wanted to see if they could smoke if they tried.

When someone comes to you in this type of situation ask him or her, "How did that first cigarette taste?" Usually they will say something like, "It tasted awful," or, "Disgusting." Tell them that if they were ever to try to smoke again, it would taste worse than they could ever imagine.

When using aversion methods like Barnyard Fun and especially with the Menudo script, always have a trash can within reach. A trashcan with a plastic liner is best. Some clients will react strongly enough to an aversion method that it will cause them to experience significant physical responses (vomiting). When a client reacts even close to that extent, then you've achieved your goal and can back off.

THE BARNYARD FUN SCRIPT

Now, I don't know if you've ever been in a barnyard. Lots of people have. Even people who have never been in a barnyard have a pretty good idea of what they might find there. Lots of different animals can be found in a barnyard, like goats or sheep or horses, even pigs. Mostly what people think of when they think of a barnyard are cattle. Cattle are probably the most common animals that we associate with a barnyard. Cattle eat a lot of grass and hay, and they drink lots of water. After they eat all of that grass and hay and drink all of that water, eventually it has to pass through their system. Wherever you find cattle in a barnyard, you find this substance that has passed through them. Now, this substance comes in a variety of shapes, sizes and consistencies. Now, some of this substance has a very high moisture content, so much so that it can't maintain any consistent shape and just flows wherever gravity takes it. Some of this substance still has a very high moisture content. Gravity still has an influence on it, but it has a bit more consistency, like mud. Some of this substance has a much lower moisture content and maintains a very consistent shape. Some of this substance is very dry; however, it maintains a very consistent shape, although any contact with it would easily break it up. There is yet more that is very dry and has no consistent shape at all, more like sawdust. This is the consistency we are interested in. This consistency is like that stuff in cigarettes. In fact, it's the same as that stuff in cigarettes.

Just experience yourself gathering up some of this substance [manure/cow shit, *etc.*] and roll it up in a piece of paper. And now light the end of that paper. You can smell that smell. Burning manure has got to smell horrible, and you can smell that smell. As you put that smoldering manure cigarette up to your face, your nose begins to burn and itch and run. Your eyes begin to burn and water. As you put that manure cigarette to your lips and take a drag, you can taste that dry, dirty, disgusting taste in your mouth. That's got to taste horrible. As the smoke begins to enter your throat, your throat begins to burn and get scratchy and raw and you start to cough and gag. As the smoke flows into your lungs, your lungs begin to burn and your lungs are repulsed and you start to convulse and choke and cough uncontrollably. You're bent over now, coughing and choking and gasping for air. The more you cough, the more your lungs burn, and the harder your lungs try to expel the disgusting substance. The smoke still drifts up and continues to burn your nose and eyes, and your eyes water, and your nose runs and itches, and you sneeze uncontrollably. You can smell that smell, smell that smell. Your mouth is salivating and you spit and cough to get that repulsive substance out. Your lungs are on fire and you're bent over trying to get your breath and you're getting dizzy and your legs are getting rubbery.

You're tough, you're determined, and you put that manure cigarette back to your lips; and you can smell that smell, smell that smell, and it burns your nose and it burns your eyes, and your nose runs, and your eyes water and itch, you sneeze, and you smell that smell, and it makes you nauseous. As you drag on that manure cigarette, you taste that taste, and smell that smell, and it burns your throat, and then it burns your lungs, and your lungs are repulsed, and you cough and choke and gasp uncontrollably. The more you cough and gasp, the more your lungs are just set on fire. You're bent over gasping and choking. It makes you dizzy, it makes you nauseous, it makes you sick, and you smell that smell, and you taste that taste, and it's disgusting, and you avoid it. You won't allow any manure cigarette near you, and you know if someone tries to offer you a cigarette, you know that they are just trying to fool you into taking one of those manure cigarettes so they can laugh at you coughing and choking. You won't allow that smoke near you, because you can smell that smell, and taste that taste, and you always keep some distance between you and that smoke, because you can smell that smell, and taste that taste, and you do anything to avoid it.

What you really want is some clean fresh water and some clean fresh air. It feels so good to just breathe fresh clean air and drink clean refreshing water.

[When working with smokeless tobacco, reverse the barnyard fun. Start with the dry manure, and work to the very moist, and have them put it in their tobacco can, and, well, you get the picture.]

Menudo 16

This is the basis for a script that you can use for clients who want to stop drinking (mainly alcohol, but it could be sodas or whatever). This is from a true story that was told to me by a friend who had witnessed the whole thing. (He no longer eats menudo.) While working with clients, this story came back to me and I decided to incorporate it into a script. There is no need to soft sell this one. You can easily (and do!) insert your client into this scene as the first drinker. You can have them realize what has happened after it's too late. They become ill. Mock it up as much as possible.

THE MENUDO SCRIPT

A friend of mine was at a party. Food was being served outdoors. Lots of beer, wine and tequila were being served up in large plastic cups. Some people were having more than enough to drink and eat. One fellow—maybe it was you—was talking with my friend and was becoming quite intoxicated. At one point, [he/you] set down the large plastic cup (which was about one-quarter full at this point) that [he/you] had been drinking from, while [he/you] went to the restroom. While [he was/you were] gone, another fellow that had been overindulging even more had also been enjoying a lot of menudo. Menudo is a soup that some ethnic people enjoy and it is made from tripe, which is the stomach lining often from an ox or sheep. (If you've ever seen it in the store, it looks quite gross, like brains or something.) This man was becoming very queasy, very quickly. He was quickly becoming desperate to find a restroom or something to throw up in. A certain large plastic cup was beginning to look very handy. He vomited the contents of his stomach into the cup (menudo, booze, and all). So now the cup contains the small amount of liquor that was left in it, along with the menudo, wine, beer, tequila and the other contents of the second gentleman's stomach. Soon our first inebriated friend—actually you—returned from the restroom, and, being unaware of what had just taken place, [he/you] picked up his large plastic cup and resumed drinking from [his/your] familiar cup. After quickly chugging down the contents of the cup, it takes a moment before it begins to dawn on [him/you] what has just occurred. As the message begins to sink into the brain, [his/your] stomach begins to churn and [he begins/you begin] to turn green. Now [he is/you are] frantically looking for a place to vomit. There is no time and [he begins/you begin] to projectile vomit uncontrollably. [He tries/You try] to control it, but [he/you] cannot. Heaving, heaving uncontrollably. People are moving away; it's making them feel nauseous as well. Even friends, who would like to help, cannot, and begin to move away as well. Who knows what people must be thinking?

Soon [he has/you have] vomited the entire contents of [his/your] stomach. Now [he has/you have] the dry heaves. Heaving, heaving, [he almost wishes/you almost wish] there was something in the stomach; somehow, it would make it easier. [His/Your] head is spinning;

[he's/you're] weak, [he's/you're] dizzy, [his/your] head is spinning. Chills run up and down [his/your] spine. [He's/You're] trembling and shaking. These are the only feelings and sensations [he associates/you associate] with drinking from now on. [He/You] can't even get near a drink now without thinking of the menudo, and the dizziness, and vomiting. [He'll/You'll] do anything to avoid it.

Scripts Tear-Out Section

No Suggestion Suggestion

At some point I'm going to be giving you a suggestion. At some point I'm going to be giving you a suggestion, a very special, a very powerful suggestion, so powerful in fact that this suggestion is effective one hundred percent of the time. Very few people have ever received this very special, very powerful suggestion. However, because of some of the things that you said during the interview process, I now know that you are ready, willing, and able to receive this suggestion, fully and completely, body, mind and spirit. *Now,* there is a side effect to this suggestion, and that side effect is that you won't even remember this suggestion. It doesn't matter that you won't remember this suggestion, because I'm going to slip in this suggestion in such a way that you won't even notice it. It doesn't matter that you won't remember this suggestion because your subconscious mind knows this suggestion. Yes, your subconscious mind knows this suggestion and your subconscious mind enjoys this suggestion. And because your subconscious mind enjoys this suggestion, your subconscious mind embraces this suggestion. Because your subconscious mind embraces this suggestion, good, healthy, positive changes occur in your life, not the least of which is [*insert client specifics here, such as,* "you are a non-smoker for the rest of your life," *or,* "you are free of that unwanted emotional baggage," *or,* "you have greater confidence," *or you can even leave it unspecified*], all because of this one very special, very powerful suggestion that I'm going to give you at some point, that you won't even remember.

Now, other good, healthy, positive changes will occur as well, all because of this one very special, very powerful suggestion and something I refer to as the domino effect. Yes, any time we take control in our lives just as you are doing right this very moment by [*insert client specifics here, or say nothing at all*], it's as if you are knocking over that first domino and the rest of the dominos begin to topple and other good, healthy, positive changes begin to fall right into your life. Some of these good, healthy, positive changes will be fairly obvious like [*client specific, or not*]. You have a great deal more energy. You feel like doing more vigorous, more active kinds of things and you do do more vigorous, more active kinds of things. You think more clearly. You have a new, more positive attitude, a new optimism; you're always looking ahead to each new day, knowing that good things are coming your way. You blaze the trail for others to follow. Yes, you set the example that others follow.

Now, other good, healthy, positive changes will occur as well, and I'm not even sure what some of these changes might be. I'd only be speculating and most likely so would you. However, it's nice to know that the subconscious mind knows exactly which good, healthy, positive changes you're up for and in what order they need to occur. It's nice to know that consciously there's not much you need to think about. There's not much you need to do. It's nice to know that the subconscious mind just takes care of everything.

Now, some of these changes may occur on a fairly subtle level. And you may be someone who is aware on a subtle level, or perhaps the hypnosis helps you to be more aware on a subtle level; it really doesn't matter at all. As you may know, sometimes things that occur on a subtle level have a very profound effect upon us—body, mind and spirit. All because of this one very special, very powerful suggestion and the domino effect.

No Suggestion Suggestion
(Smoking)

At some point I'm going to be giving you a suggestion. At some point I'm going to be giving you a suggestion, a very special, a very powerful suggestion, so powerful in fact that this suggestion is effective one hundred percent of the time. Very few people have ever received this very special, very powerful suggestion. However, because of some of the things that you said during the interview process, I now know that you are ready, willing and able to receive this suggestion, fully and completely, body, mind and spirit. *Now,* there is a side effect to this suggestion, and that side effect is that you won't even remember this suggestion. It doesn't matter that you won't remember this suggestion, because I'm going to slip in this suggestion in such a way that you won't even notice it. It doesn't matter that you won't remember this suggestion because your subconscious mind knows this suggestion. Yes, your subconscious mind knows this suggestion and your subconscious mind enjoys this suggestion. And because your subconscious mind enjoys this suggestion, your subconscious mind embraces this suggestion. Because your subconscious mind embraces this suggestion, good, healthy, positive changes occur in your life, not the least of which is the fact that you are a non-smoker for the rest of your life, never again desiring cigarettes or tobacco in any form. All because of this one very special, very powerful suggestion that I'm going to give you at some point, that you won't even remember.

Now, other good, healthy, positive changes will occur as well, all because of this one very special, very powerful suggestion and something I refer to as the domino effect. Yes, any time we take control in our lives just as you are doing right this very moment by becoming a non-smoker for the rest of your life, it's as if you are knocking over that first domino and the rest of the dominos begin to topple and other good, healthy, positive changes begin to fall right into your life. Some of these good, healthy, positive changes will be fairly obvious, like you are a non-smoker for the rest of your life. You breathe more easily. You feel better about yourself and who you are. You have a great deal more energy. You feel like doing more vigorous, more active kinds of things and you do do more vigorous, more active kinds of things. You think more clearly. You have a new, more positive attitude, a new optimism; you're always looking ahead to each new day, knowing that good things are coming your way. You blaze the trail for others to follow. Yes, you set the example that others follow.

Now, other good, healthy, positive changes will occur as well. Some of these changes may or may not have anything to do with being a non-smoker and I'm not even sure what some of these changes might be. I'd only be speculating and most likely so would you. However, it's nice to know that the subconscious mind knows exactly which good, healthy, positive changes you're up for and in what order they need to occur. It's nice to know that consciously there's not much you need to think about. There's not much you need to do. It's nice to know that the subconscious mind just takes care of everything and good, healthy, positive changes come to you.

Now, some of these changes may occur on a fairly subtle level. And you may be someone who is aware on a subtle level, or perhaps the hypnosis helps you to be more aware on a subtle level; it really doesn't matter at all. As you may know, sometimes things that occur on a subtle level have a very profound effect upon us, body, mind and spirit. All because of this one very special, very powerful suggestion and the domino effect.

As a result, your new non-smoking lifestyle becomes a compulsion for you. Not only are you a non-smoker, you take control of your life in other ways as well—like the kinds of nutrients you put in your body. You know the value of maintaining a healthy diet and in the proper quantities. Exercise is a similar kind of thing. You know the value of living an active lifestyle. And now as a non-smoker you have a great deal more energy and you feel like doing more vigorous, more active kinds of things, and you do do more vigorous, more active kinds of things.

You take time out for yourself as well—time to do your own things, time to have your own thoughts and feelings, time to just kick back and relax. And you're very relaxed right this very moment and you can only be this relaxed as a non-smoker. No one could be this relaxed and smoking at the same time, and you are this relaxed, and you are a non-smoker. And because you are this relaxed, all of the suggestions take complete and thorough effect upon you, body, mind and spirit.

No Suggestion Follow-Up

[You will give (read) this piece of patter to your client near the end of the session.]

You may remember any of this session you wish to remember, with the one exception of that one very special, very powerful suggestion that I gave you at some time that you won't even remember. It doesn't matter that you won't remember that suggestion, for it's the effects of that suggestion upon you that are important and the effects of that suggestion will follow you day by day, body, mind and spirit. Now, you might wonder about that suggestion. You might think about that suggestion. You may even try and remember that suggestion; however, it will just make the suggestion more powerful and you will still not be able to remember it.

No Suggestion Connect

[Often, in following sessions, I use the No Suggestion Connect with a client who has previously been given the No Suggestion Suggestion. This could happen during the client's next session a week or so apart, or I've even used it months or years later. The wording is something like the following.]

The last time we were together, I gave you a suggestion, a very special suggestion. That suggestion has continued to work on you mind, body and spirit, and that's probably one reason why you are here today. Today, I'm going to give you another suggestion, a different suggestion, but a somewhat similar suggestion. Because I'll be giving you this suggestion now and because I gave you that suggestion then, both suggestions become more powerful than they could have ever become on their own. Sometimes adding one and one together ends up being a lot more than two, something I refer to as compounding, and both suggestions become many times more powerful than they ever could have on their own.

[Follow this with other suggestion work.]

Choices

We live in a world of choices, and choices are a good thing. Choices are what give us freedom and the ability to be unique and creative individuals. Without choices we would all just be clones of one another.

When it comes to food and exercise there are lots and lots of choices we can make. Perhaps you find yourself going to restaurants or fast food places from time to time. When I was a youngster, going to a restaurant was a really big deal, because it happened so infrequently. So, of course, everyone wanted to order his or her favorites and get dessert if possible, because you never knew when that was going to happen again. Back then it probably wasn't such a big issue, because food was different and lifestyles were different and it happened so infrequently that it wasn't a big factor in our health. Nowadays, due to our speeded up hurry-here-hurry-there lifestyles, restaurants and fast food places have become more a part of our normal routines. We can no longer afford to treat each trip to a restaurant or fast food place as if it were a special occasion. Some restaurants have lots and lots of choices that we can make and usually this is a good thing. The more choices there are, the more opportunities there are to make good, healthy, intelligent choices. It feels good to make those good, healthy, intelligent choices that put you in control. At first it may seem a little strange eating so much differently than others around you, like people you might be dining with or just people sitting about the restaurant. But soon it seems strange to eat in any other way. Your positive eating choices help to influence others in a positive way as well. Other people begin to notice that you are eating differently. Not only do they notice that you are eating differently, they notice a difference in you, which may influence them to make better, healthier choices, as well.

Other people have what I refer to as that cattle herd mentality. In the cattle herd, that's where everyone just does the same things that everyone else does. Well, there may be some warm fuzzies in that, but when everyone does the same thing that everyone else does, then everyone gets pretty much the same results that everyone else gets, and when you look out there that can be pretty scary.

You, however, are someone who is willing to think outside of the box. You are someone who is willing to try something different. I know that because you are here today and that's the sort of action a person takes who's willing to think outside the box, and do something different. That's what people do who make a difference in their lives, a difference in the world. You make a difference by doing something different. Doing the same old things only gives the same results; it's only by doing something different that we can make a difference, a difference in our lives, a difference in the world. It feels good to make the good, healthy, intelligent choices that make a difference for you.

Some restaurants and fast food places have fewer choices than others; however, some choices are still better than others. It feels good to make the good, healthy, intelligent choices that put you in control. *Now*, at some restaurants and fast food places there may be so few choices or such poor choices that sometimes it's better to make no choice at all, than to make a poor choice. You know a poor choice could mean a setback and you avoid any type of setbacks, for you desire to keep moving ahead in a positive direction. And you know that somewhere, shortly down the road, there will be an opportunity to make good, healthy, intelligent choices that put you in control. It feels good to make the good, healthy, intelligent choices that put you in control.

The grocery store is another place where we get to make choices. At the grocery store there are lots and lots of choices that we could make. And this is a good thing, because the more choices there are, the more opportunities there are to make good, healthy, intelligent choices that put you in control. It feels good to make those good, healthy, intelligent choices that put you in control. There have been times when you were in the grocery store and you made some good, healthy, intelligent choices that put you in control and it feels good. You know what I mean. There have been times when you made good, healthy, intelligent choices that put you in control and it feels good. And when you make the good, healthy, intelligent choices that put you in control, you are in control. You are in control of your health. You are in control of your aliveness. You are in control of your body. You are in control of the way you look and feel. It feels good to make the good, healthy, intelligent choices that put you in control.

On the other hand, there have been times when you made a poor choice, and you knew you were making a poor choice. You made a poor choice; you knew it was a poor choice; yet you continued to make the poor choice. As a result you feel guilty, embarrassed, discouraged, disgusted, uncomfortable and out of control. You hate feeling out of control. You hate feeling uncomfortable, yet there you are. You made a poor choice; you knew it was a poor choice. As a result you feel guilty, embarrassed, discouraged, disgusted, uncomfortable and out of control. You hate feeling out of control. You hate feeling uncomfortable. As a result you can't even enjoy the poor choice. Yes, you've added insult to injury; you've poured salt in your own wound. You made a poor choice. You knew it was a poor choice. As a result you feel guilty, embarrassed, discouraged, disgusted, uncomfortable and out of control. These awful feelings and sensations take away from any enjoyment you might have gotten from that poor choice. Not only is there no enjoyment from that poor choice, you've wasted good money, and you put poison into your body. What could be worse than that? How awful is that?

From now on you can't even get near one of those poor choices without feeling guilty, embarrassed, discouraged, disgusted, uncomfortable and out of control. You hate feeling out of control. You hate feeling uncomfortable. There you are in the grocery store, pushing your cart down the aisle, and you're right near one of those poor choices. You can feel the guilty, embarrassing, discouraging, uncomfortable, out of control sensations gushing right up through your body. You feel guilty, embarrassed, discouraged, disgusted, uncomfortable, out of control. *It feels awful!* The best thing, the best thing that you can do, is to quickly move away, and quickly go make some good, healthy, positive, intelligent choices that put you in control. It feels good to make the good, healthy, positive, intelligent choices that put you in control. When you make the good, healthy, positive, intelligent choices that put you in control, you are in control. You are in control of your health; you are in control of your body. You are in control of the way you look and feel. It feels good to make the good, healthy, positive, intelligent choices that put you in control.

When it comes to exercise, there are lots and lots of good, healthy, positive, intelligent choices you can make. Some of these choices are simple little things you can do every day, like using the stairs instead of the elevator or escalator. Or park your car further away when you are at the grocery store or the shopping mall or at work. Not only is parking further away a simple way to add a little exercise into our daily routine, we are taking better care of our vehicle at the same time. And walk to the convenience store or other places instead of driving. Every little thing we do like this is helpful toward making us leaner and healthier. It feels good to make the good, healthy, intelligent choices that put you in control.

Chaos

In the southern central portion of the north mainly in the panhandle, it's about as round as a perfect square can be and still remain perpendicular. Up until then nothing was really normal except the sight of the air, when things were really noisy, and there was the crunching of numbers to cause consideration. It was easier to *let go of all that weight* and let it sink to the ceiling, like *in no time at all*. Only the ones with two or more on the left had a good sense of sideways. Mostly party members. Other joiners *become fit as well*. Meandering as if it were no effort at all. Even toppling upright seemed to have a positive effect. Especially during the night light or after. It was easier to *just lighten up*. No more sinking sensations. It only happened at those odd times anyway. So you have that to look forward to. Even though you may not remember when it finally does happen, isn't it strange when *it works* that way? So you have that to look forward to, even though you may not remember when it finally does happen. Isn't it strange when *it works* that way? There is no struggle of course when that does happen. And you *become firm* each time. You've had that happen before. I noticed that about you a number of times in the past when you thought no one was paying attention. You may have thought you weren't being noticed. Some certainly did not. It flows both ways, just like snow up the hill. On the other side it's smooth and you *become light on your feet* it's easier than carrying that weight up the hill. Soaking up the light sensations below. Afterwards it seems to make sense, especially the movement, you can't cross your legs in that position anyway it feels better to *stretch out first*. I learned that years before in adulthood. Funny how that could make sense and something about floating weightless happens even when *you try harder. You can be firm* about that most are. It happens when you most expect and sometimes more. There's no need to not wonder why. It crosses over into familiar territory, if you follow what I mean, not that I could ever be mean. It's just more comfortable to uncross legs sometimes. Other parts work easier this time of year as well and not just during the day. You've probably hovered around that issue a time or two. It can be good as things *change for the better.* What once weighed heavily now evaporates easily into thin. Most forms of transportation rarely do that, although *things can be different in the future.* They dug a big hole just to support the feeling light. It worked better than that old prop. Throats get dry that way and *action is necessary.* Who could foresee that? And not just in the suburbs if you know what I mean. It doesn't matter what the weather is doing, it's always a good time to—*do that.* It's nuts to think it couldn't *work out* just in that way. You're in control. I know that because you are here right now. How could it be different? Everyone else goes down that other stone road, just like it was a field. Some people learned it in school, you'll just have to ... Be smart enough ... to *do it on your own.* Midway between you get off way ahead, I couldn't tell you more. It seemed strange to me too until we ... *Find that change*—there's no substitute for that. You planted the seed, you know what is happening as *it dwindles away.* You may have had it happen before, just not as easily. It happens that way only *easier now.* That other time can just *let go now.* You have a mind of your own and no one else can change it. You already know what you want. You know what you will do. Even if for just 59 seconds anyone can do 59 seconds. You know you are just right *now.* It's the best time *now.* Later could be too late. It's never cloudy then. Only good happens *now.* What once was fuzzy and fluffy is now *firm and smooth.* Mostly there is no need to be too deep. It works well both ways. There's no time like the present regardless of what happened before. You're not the same person as then. *You have a mind of your own* and you have set it. It feels good to move from one thing to the next. *The body enjoys movement.* It's good to have those choices and there are lots of choices, *you know the right choices,* I don't even need to tell you that. It feels better to make the right choices. It takes such a weight off. It's just so much easier that way. Not like struggling the wrong way. That happened before, no longer. Mostly sunny now. You can see through the haze. The body enjoys feeling healthy. Outside and feel the light. *Light meals.* Whenever. You're going to be there anyway. It's barely abstract, bituminous perhaps. Some smaller cities are that way. One can only imagine. It's not to say it smelled some way or different all together. Whatever and whichever it doesn't seem to make any difference, each day is and every way things seem to work in your favor. No matter where you are or what you may be doing you find things *work in your favor.* It's nice to know wherever you are whatever you might be doing things are working in your favor; you have control of *feeling good about yourself.* No matter who might be around or what you might be doing, *it feels good to take care of yourself first.* You don't mind being different from others, that's how you make a difference in you.

FULL

There have been times, everybody has had times. You have had times. I have had times. Everybody has had times, times when you've just had way, way, way too much. You know what I mean, times when you have just had way, way, way too much to eat. Perhaps there have been some family gatherings, like Thanksgiving or Christmas or a wedding reception, or some other celebration where there is just lots and lots of food—you know, what some people might refer to as a spread. I guess we've all had the feelings, sensations, ideas or thoughts that, wow, it all looks so good, I think I'll just try a little bit of everything. You know, by the time you've tried a little bit of everything, it's just way, way, way too much. You know what I mean. You probably find yourself drifting back to a particular incident where you've just had way, way, way too much to eat. You know how it feels. You can feel it in your body right this very moment. You feel full, stuffed, heavy, sluggish, slow, bloated and sloth-like. You hate feeling bloated; you hate feeling uncomfortable. You probably wonder why? Why did I ever think this was a good idea? You might wish you could turn back time, but you cannot. You feel full, stuffed, heavy, sluggish, slow, bloated and sloth-like. You hate feeling bloated, you hate feeling uncomfortable. One more bite, one more bite would be enough to put you over the edge, to cause you to explode, or become violently ill. You probably feel a bit nauseous right now. You feel full, stuffed, heavy, sluggish, slow, bloated and sloth-like. You hate feeling bloated; you hate feeling uncomfortable. You might feel a bit embarrassed; yes, your stomach is so pooched out there is nothing you can do to hide it, and who knows who might be noticing. You probably find yourself loosening your clothing a bit, trying to get some kind of relief, but even that doesn't help all that much. You feel full, stuffed, heavy, sluggish, slow, bloated and sloth-like. You hate feeling bloated; you hate feeling uncomfortable. You might notice that you have difficulty breathing. Yes, your stomach is so full that your diaphragm can no longer expand properly and all you get are these short little breaths of air. You might even feel a bit vulnerable. Yes, if there were some kind of an emergency, you don't know if you could move fast enough to save yourself, let alone help anyone else. All you really want to do is kick back and relax and wait for these awful feelings and sensations to go away, but it just takes forever. You feel full, stuffed, heavy, sluggish, slow, bloated and sloth-like. You hate feeling bloated; you hate feeling uncomfortable. You will do anything to avoid these awful feelings and sensations. From now on, you notice these sensations come on so much more quickly, so much more easily now. Sometimes all it takes is a bite or two or three and you feel full, stuffed, heavy, sluggish, slow, bloated and sloth-like. You hate feeling bloated; you hate feeling uncomfortable. You will do anything to avoid these awful feelings and sensations.

There are certain times when these awful feelings and sensations come on so much more quickly, so much more easily than before. For instance, perhaps you find yourself wandering into the kitchen when you're not even hungry. Perhaps you've eaten not that long ago, but there you are, poking through the cupboards or the refrigerator or the counters. You find yourself looking for that one little morsel that is going to make the world all right. From now on, all it takes is one little bite, one little cookie, one little cracker or potato chip, one little bite of chocolate or ice cream or candy or any sort of sweet or salty or fatty or carbohydratie or snacky item to put you right over the edge. To put you right into those full, stuffed, heavy, sluggish, slow, bloated and sloth-like sensations that you despise. You hate feeling bloated; you hate feeling uncomfortable; you'll do anything to avoid them. From now on, you can't even think about what might be in that kitchen when you're not hungry. You can't look in those cupboards or refrigerator without feeling full, stuffed, heavy, sluggish, slow, bloated and sloth-like. You hate feeling bloated; you hate feeling uncomfortable. You'll do anything to avoid these awful feelings and sensations. And the best thing that you can do to avoid these awful feelings and sensations is to eat very … very … slowly … and cautiously. For you know how quickly, how easily, these full, stuffed, heavy, sluggish, slow, bloated and sloth-like sensations can come creeping up on you. You hate feeling bloated; you hate feeling uncomfortable. At the first sign, at the very first sign of any sensations of satisfaction, you discontinue eating. You push your plate away. You put your food down. You are done. You don't mind, you don't mind at all that there is still food left. You know you are not wasting food. The only way that you can waste food is to put food into your body when you are not even hungry. Then it goes to waste, it goes to your waist, and you don't need to waste food in that manner; you don't need it to go to your waist. Now, if there's quite a bit of food left over, you might put it in a container and save it for later, or throw it in the trash or the compost. You don't mind. You don't mind at all. For you know you are not wasting food. The only way that you can waste food is to put food into your body when you are not truly hungry and then it goes to waste, it goes to your waist, and you don't need it going to your waist. Now, if there's quite a bit of food left over you might put it in a container and save it for later, or throw it in the trash or the compost. You don't mind. You don't mind at all. For you know you are not wasting food. The only way that you can waste food is to put food into your body when you are not truly hungry and then it goes to waste, it goes to your waist, and you don't need it going to your waist. You don't mind, you don't mind at all that there is still food left on your plate, for you are not a child, you are not a child and no one can make you clean your plate. You are not a child and no one can make you clean your plate. You are an adult. You are not a child and no one can make you clean your plate. In fact you are an adult and you defy, you defy *anyone* to make you clean your plate. You defy *anyone* to make you clean your plate by always leaving food on your plate. Sometimes you leave half the plate of food, or even more depending on how you feel; other times it's just a few bites or so. You always leave food on your plate, just to show that you are the one who is in control, that you are defiant. Sometimes you leave half the plate of food or even more depending on how you feel; other times it's just a few bites or so. You always leave food on your plate, just to show that you are the one who is in control, that you are defiant. And it helps in another way as well because it helps you to avoid those full, stuffed, heavy, sluggish, slow, bloated and sloth-like sensations. You hate feeling bloated; you hate feeling uncomfortable. You'll do anything to avoid these awful feelings and sensations. On the other hand, there have been times when you were a bit on the empty side and it feels good. You know what I mean. There were times when you were a youngster and you are playing outside and it's near dinnertime and you're a bit on the empty side; but you don't mind, you don't mind at all. You're having way too much fun just playing and being active. You don't mind that you're a bit on the empty side. It feels good. You feel light, alive, energetic and enthusiastic. It feels good. Somewhere in the back of your mind is the hope, the desire, that your mother or someone will not be calling you in for dinner, because you're having way too much fun just playing and being active. You don't mind that you're a bit on the empty side. It feels good. You feel light, alive, energetic and enthusiastic. It feels good. And if your mother or someone does call you in for dinner, you pretend as though you never heard a thing. You ignore their calls because you're having way too much fun just playing and being active. You don't mind that you're a bit on the empty side. It feels good. You feel light, alive, energetic and enthusiastic. It feels good.

If your mother or someone is finally successful at getting you to come in for dinner, you just do the obligatory. You eat a few bites of this and that, just to satisfy them, so that you can excuse yourself from the table and get right back out to playing and being active. As you leave the table you don't mind at all that you are still a bit on the empty side. You don't mind at all because you feel light, alive, energetic and enthusiastic. It feels good. It feels so much better than those full, stuffed, heavy, sluggish, slow, bloated and sloth-like sensations that you despise. You would rather feel light, alive, energetic and enthusiastic. It feels good.

Stairs for Metabolism

Ten—Feel yourself beginning to move down the stairs.

Nine—Feel yourself going deeper and deeper.

Eight—Moving further down the stairs, closer to that special place; your special place of comfort, relaxation and safety; that special place where today we are *cranking up the metabolism.* Yes, we're *speeeeeeeeding up the metabolism,* so that each bite of food, each calorie, each gram of fat, each bit of carbohydrate that enters into your system is burned up thoroughly and completely and converted into heat and energy for the body. As a result, you're more alive, energetic and enthusiastic. The pounds melt away like butter on a hot summer's day.

Seven—Going deeper and deeper and deeper down, feeling more relaxed even than before.

Six—Going deeper and deeper inside.

Five—Moving further down the stairs, closer to that special place; your special place of comfort, relaxation and safety; that special place where today we are *cranking up the metabolism.* Yes, we're *speeeeeeeeding up the metabolism,* so that each bite of food, each calorie, each gram of fat, each bit of carbohydrate that enters into your system is burned up thoroughly and completely and converted into heat and energy for the body. As a result, you're more alive, energetic and enthusiastic. The pounds melt away like butter on a hot summer's day.

Four—Moving further down the stairs, going deeper and deeper down.

Three—Going deeper and deeper inside.

Two—Almost down the stairs now, almost to that special place;

your special place of comfort, relaxation and safety; that special place where today we are *cranking up the metabolism.* Yes, we're *speeeeeeeeding up the metabolism,* so that each bite of food, each calorie, each gram of fat, each bit of carbohydrate that enters into your system is burned up thoroughly and completely and converted into heat and energy for the body. As a result, you're more alive, energetic and enthusiastic. The pounds melt away like butter on a hot summer's day.

One—All the way down the stairs now, all the way to that special place; your special place of comfort, relaxation and safety; that special place that is just right for you.

Notice that door or gate. Notice how big it is. Notice what shape it is. Notice what it's made of. Is it iron, is it wood, or is it some other material? Now reach out and touch that door or gate. Notice how it feels. Is it rough, or is it smooth? Is it warm, or is it cool? Now push open that door or gate and walk through into your special place, your special place of comfort, safety and relaxation.

Notice what you see or feel. Notice the temperature of the air on your skin. Notice what kind of day it is. Is the sun shining? Is the sky blue? Are there clouds?

Notice any sounds. Perhaps there are the sounds of water, or a gentle breeze, or some other comforting sounds. Perhaps it's just the peace and quiet.

Notice any smells. This is your special place and it's just right for you. And you can come here anytime you want, any time at all, to just relax, to be creative, or to solve some problem. It's your special place and it's just right for you. Now take a deep breath and breathe in all of these good feelings and sensations. Breathe them in to every cell of your body.

Metabolism

Experience yourself looking at yourself. Experience yourself looking at yourself, and you are going to begin by focusing on the area from your waist up. To be more specific, you are going to start by focusing on the area of your head. And to be even more specific than that, you are going to begin by focusing in on the area of your mouth and jaw. As you focus in on the area of your own mouth and jaw, it's just like looking through an X-ray. And, just like looking through an X-ray, you can see all of the inner workings of the mouth and jaw area. You can see the jawbones, the jaw muscles, the teeth, the tongue, and all of the interrelated parts—just like looking through an X-ray. Now, experience yourself putting a bite of food into your mouth and, just like in an X-ray, you can see the bite of food entering your mouth. Soon you begin to chew the bite of food. And, just like in an X-ray, you can see the teeth chewing and grinding away at the bite of food. And, just like in an X-ray, you can see the jawbones moving up and down and the jaw muscles expanding and contracting, the tongue pushing the bite of food this way and that for maximum efficiency. You notice you take your time; you take a good, long time, and chew each bite of food slowly and completely. For as you know, the mouth, the teeth are the first part of the digestive system and it's important that you chew each bite slowly and completely. You notice that when you chew each bite slowly and completely you gain a great deal more satisfaction from each bite. Yes, because you chew each bite slowly and completely, you gain much more enjoyment from each bite of food and you feel more easily satisfied. You notice you stop eating sooner because you feel more satisfied.

Now experience yourself swallowing that bite of food and, just like in an X-ray, you can see the bite of food moving down the esophagus. As the bite of food moves further and further down the esophagus it gets closer and closer to the stomach, and as it gets closer and closer to the stomach you begin to notice something. You begin to notice that it is like there's a furnace in the stomach, and there's a fire in the furnace in the stomach. As the bite of food reaches the end of the esophagus it drops into the furnace in the stomach and into the flames of the fire in the furnace in the stomach. The bite of food becomes fuel for the flames of the fire in the furnace in the stomach. You begin to notice something else. You notice that the flames of the fire in the furnace in the stomach are not all that great. And you begin to notice something else and that is that there is a dial on the side of the furnace in the stomach. You notice that the dial is marked from low to high. And you notice that the dial is set more toward the low side. So just experience yourself beginning to turn that dial up. As you turn that dial up, the flames begin to grow. The flames get larger and larger and more air is introduced into the furnace and the flames get hotter and hotter and larger and larger. Keep turning that dial up until the flames begin to *roar* and you can feel the heat pouring off the flames of the fire in the furnace in the stomach. Now each bite of food that drops into the flames of the fire in the furnace in the stomach is burned up completely and converted into heat and energy for the body. Each calorie, each gram of fat, each bit of carbohydrate is burned up thoroughly and completely and converted into heat and energy for the body. Every bite of food, every calorie, each gram of fat, every bit of carbohydrate is burned up thoroughly and completely and converted into heat and energy for your body. Yes, that's right, every bite of food, every calorie, every gram of fat, every bit of carbohydrate is burned up thoroughly and completely and converted into heat and energy for the body. You begin to notice something else. You begin to notice that there is plumbing running through the furnace in the stomach. This plumbing is the circulatory system. The blood flows through the plumbing in the furnace in the stomach to pick up heat and energy for the body. The blood flowing through the plumbing is becoming super-heated and super-energized, which means we need to compensate for that; it means we need to speed up the flow of the circulatory system; and that means we need to speed up the pumping mechanism, *the heart*. Just bring your attention to the area of your own heart and imagine a large pumping mechanism working away. It could be one of those old steam driven pumps that just seems to run on and on forever; or it could be an oil field pump that runs day after day, year after year, on and on endlessly. Or it could be any type of pumping mechanism that you might imagine. Notice that there is a dial on the side of the pumping mechanism. This dial on the side of the pump is marked from low to high. Once again, you need to turn the dial up, but just a little bit this time, just enough to increase the flow slightly. So begin to turn that dial up until the pump starts pumping a bit faster—that's right, right about there. Now see, feel, experience, notice that pumping mechanism running just a bit more quickly. And see, feel, notice the blood flowing through the circulatory system just a bit more quickly. Now there are lots of different kinds of pumps, but all pumps work in one of two ways. Some pumps pump a lot of pressure, like the pump you would use to pump up your car tire. That pump pumps a lot of pressure. Other pumps don't pump much pressure; they work by drawing fluid through a line, much like you would suck water through a straw. And that's the kind of pumping mechanism you have here. Even though you've increased the flow, the pressure in the lines remains the same. It's just moving through the lines more quickly.

If you are someone who has experienced an imbalance in the pressure in your lines, there is a valve on the pump (much like a faucet for the hose on the side of a house) with a gauge. If you want to turn the pressure in the lines down, turn the valve in a clockwise manner. If you want to turn the pressure up, turn the valve in a counterclockwise manner. Watch the gauge until the pressure is right where you desire. It doesn't take much to adjust the pressure to where you desire.

As the blood flows through the plumbing in the furnace in the stomach, it picks up the heat and energy from the fire in the furnace in the stomach and it begins to carry this super-warmed, super-energized blood throughout the body. This super-warmed, super-energized blood is also a super-healing blood. As the blood flows, it flows into the internal organs creating a super-warm, super-energized, tingling sensation, rinsing away any toxins, any unwanted particles, any discolorations, any discomfort, any disease; rinsing it away and flushing it away, out through the body's natural filtration system.

As the blood begins to flow towards the extremities, it flows up into the neck and throat and into the cranial area, again rinsing away any toxins, any unwanted particles, any discomforts, any disease, all throughout the cranial area, leaving behind a super-warm, super-healing and tingling sensation throughout the cranial area, right to the very cells of the scalp.

As the blood flows toward the outer extremities, it begins flowing through the shoulders and out into the arms. You can just feel the warm healing fluid moving through your shoulder muscles and shoulder joints, rinsing away any toxins, any unwanted particles, any impurities, any discomforts, any disease; rinsing them away, flushing them away, leaving behind a super-warming, super-energized, healing, tingling sensation. As the blood flows down through the arms, the elbows, it's rinsing away any toxins, any unwanted particles, any discolorations, any discomforts, any disease; rinsing them away, to be flushed out through the body's natural filtration system. As the blood flows into the hands and fingers, you can feel the super-warm fluid flowing into your hands and the very tips of your fingers, leaving behind a super-healing, super-warm, energized, tingling sensation. Feel that super-warm fluid filling your hands and fingers.

As the blood flows down to the lower extremities, it flows down through the hips and into the thighs. Feel that warm healing fluid flowing through your hip muscles and your hip joints, rinsing away any toxins, any unwanted particles, any impurities, any discomforts, any disease, leaving behind a super-warm, super-energized, super-healing, tingling sensation. Feel the warm healing fluid flowing down through your thighs and flowing into the knees, cleansing and healing and energizing, flowing down into the calves and shins and down through the ankles, leaving behind a super-warm, super-energized, tingling sensation.

As the blood flows into the feet and toes, feel the warm fluid flowing into your feet and toes. Notice the super-warm, super-healing, tingling sensation. Feel that super-warm fluid flowing into your feet and toes. Notice how warm and tingly your feet and toes now feel, as if you had your feet in one of those super-warm bath machines—the kind that you put your feet into the hot water and Epsom salts, and it vibrates and massages your feet in the hot water and Epsom salts. It feels so good and it's coming from the inside. Notice that super-warm, super-energized, healing, tingling sensation all throughout your entire body.

Now, something else has happened. Because we have sped up the metabolism, because we have increased the flames of the fire in the furnace in the stomach, something else has occurred. We have created a greater demand for fuel. That fuel needs to come from fuel that's been stored throughout the body in the form of fat cells. This is the job of the circulatory system as well. The blood cells flow throughout the body and pick up fat cells and carry them back to the furnace in the stomach to deposit them into the flames of the fire in the furnace in the stomach. Just experience the blood cells picking up the fat cells and carrying them back through the plumbing in the furnace in the stomach and depositing them right into the flames of the fire in the furnace in the stomach. As each fat cell drops into the flames of the fire in the furnace in the stomach, the flames *leap and crack and snap and pop with delight. You can feel the bursts of heat and energy blasting off the flames of the furnace in the stomach.* As each fat cell drops into the flames of the fire in the furnace in the stomach, the flames *leap and crack and snap and pop with delight. You can feel the bursts of heat and energy blasting off the flames of the furnace in the stomach.* There may be some areas of your body where more fat cells are stored than others, and you can just experience the blood flowing to these areas and carrying fat cells back to the flames of the fire in the furnace in the stomach. Yes, as each blood cell passes through the plumbing in the furnace in the stomach, it deposits a fat cell directly into the flames of the fire in the furnace in the stomach. As each fat cell drops into the flames of the fire in the furnace in the stomach, the flames *leap and crack and snap and pop with delight. You can feel the bursts of heat and energy blasting off the flames of the furnace in the stomach.* With every beat of your heart, with every breath you take, fat cells are being carried away to the fire in the furnace in the stomach. With every beat of your heart, with every breath you take, you're becoming slimmer, trimmer, fitter and healthier.

It's nice to know that you are in control of these dials and you can turn them up or down any time you wish, and I encourage you to do so from time to time. And it's nice to know that your body is working more efficiently, more effectively than ever. Right this very moment you're very relaxed. Even though you are very relaxed right this very moment, your body is working more effectively, more efficiently than before. When you get up at the end of this session, you will weigh less than you did when you sat down, all because your body is working more efficiently, more effectively than ever before.

And it's nice to know that no matter where you are, no matter what you are doing, your body is working more efficiently, more effectively than ever before. When you are working, performing your normal tasks, *somewhere in the back of your mind there is this gnawing, this nagging, sensation that your body is working more efficiently, more effectively, than ever before.* You can feel the pounds slipping, sliding, dripping, dropping right off your body. You feel yourself as lighter, leaner, healthier. You move more freely, more easily, more gracefully. You notice your clothing fits you differently; perhaps you're wearing different kinds of clothing altogether. You feel better about yourself and who you are— more confident. Others treat you differently, making positive comments about your lean, healthy appearance.

Perhaps you are doing other normal kinds of things like shopping, and there are lots of different kinds of shopping we can do. Perhaps you find yourself going to the shopping mall from time to time. Around the holidays, just about everyone ends up at the shopping mall sooner or later. It's amazing how much exercise we get at the shopping mall. At a shopping mall, you might be going from this store to that store, hauling packages wherever you go, picking up this or that item, checking for bargains at this store or that store, comparing an item from this store to an item at that store, running here and there trying to get ideas for this person or that person. And, actually, you are getting a lot more exercise than you might be aware of. And the whole time in the back of your mind you have this awareness—this gnawing, nagging sensation—that your body is working more efficiently, more effectively than ever before.

There are other kinds of shopping that you might do as well, like at the grocery store. There you are at the grocery store pushing your cart down the aisle and you have this certain awareness in the back of your mind—a knowing, a gnawing, a nagging sensation—that your body is working more efficiently, more effectively than ever before, which only causes you to be more conscientious and to make the smarter, healthier choices that put you in control. You know certain nutrients, certain fuels, burn more efficiently in your body. You know your metabolism is working more efficiently for you and you want to keep it that way. You buy and use only the best nutrients, the best fuels for your body, to keep your body running at its best. As you approach the checkout counter, you begin to notice the tabloids; yes, you notice the tabloids; and as you notice the tabloids, *somewhere in the back of your mind there's a knowing—a gnawing, a nagging sensation—that your body is working more efficiently, more effectively than ever before.* You can feel the pounds slipping, sliding, dripping, dropping, falling right off your body. You feel yourself as lighter, leaner, healthier and fitter. You move more freely, more quickly, more easily and more gracefully. You notice your clothing fits you differently; perhaps you're wearing different kinds of clothing altogether. You feel better about yourself and who you are—more confident. Others treat you differently, making positive comments about your lean, healthy appearance.

When you exercise, when you exercise, your body is working eight times more effectively, eight times more effectively than ever before. That means that you are burning off eight times the calories, eight times the fat cells. Now, I'm not talking about some little namby pamby exercise. I'm talking about real exercise with real effort and real intention behind it. Your body is working eight times more effectively than before, which only encourages you to do even more. Perhaps you do more repetitions, or use more resistance, or keep at it longer, or with more effort, because your body is working eight times more effectively than ever before.

When you're sleeping, you sleep comfortably through, especially because you know your body is working more efficiently, more effectively than ever before. Even while you sleep, *somewhere in the back of your mind there is this knowing—this gnawing, this nagging sensation—that your body is working more efficiently, more effectively than ever before,* and you can feel the pounds slipping, sliding, dripping, dropping, falling right off your body. You feel yourself as lighter, leaner, healthier and fitter than ever before. You have good positive dreams that help to guide you through life. A lot of these good positive dreams are about your lean, healthy, fit body and wearing the kinds of clothes you want to wear. You wake up in the morning feeling alive, alert and refreshed and all of the time that you are sleeping, your body is working more efficiently, more effectively than before. While you're asleep your body is burning fat and calories and you get up in the morning weighing less than you did when you went to bed. And no matter where you are, no matter what you might be doing, *somewhere in the back of your mind there is this knowing—this gnawing, this nagging sensation—that your body is working more efficiently, more effectively than ever before,* and you can feel the pounds slipping, sliding, dripping, dropping right off your body. You feel yourself as lighter, leaner, healthier and fitter. The pounds are just melting away like butter on a hot summer day.

Metabolism II

You might recall the last time we were together. We did some work on your metabolism. You might recall that furnace in your stomach. Just bring your attention to your stomach and that furnace in your stomach. This time it's a bit of a different furnace. This time it's a boiler furnace.

I would guess that we've all seen a movie at sometime with a steamship. Down in the bowels of that steamship is the boiler furnace room. Men are working busily down there in that boiler furnace room, shoveling scoop after scoop of coal through that boiler furnace door, heating up water to make steam for those big old steam engines. That's what's happening in your stomach right this very moment. Although it's not coal that these men are shoveling through the boiler furnace door, it's fat cells. Yes, these men are working, busily shoveling scoop after scoop of fat cells through that boiler furnace door. It's as if they are mining these fat cells from throughout your body, scoop after scoop of fat cells through that boiler furnace door. Each time they shovel a scoop full of fat cells through that boiler furnace door, the flames come licking back out at them. Their bodies glisten with sweat as they work so feverishly hard in the unbearable heat. Yet they continue shoveling scoop after scoop of fat cells through that boiler furnace door.

With each scoop of fat cells the boiler furnace is getting hotter and hotter. The heat begins to radiate throughout your body. You can feel it radiate up through your neck and throat into your cranial area. You can feel it radiate out through your shoulders, down through your arms, and into your hands and the very tips of your fingers. Feel it radiating down into your lower extremities. Feel it radiating down through your hips into your thighs, through your knees and calves and shins. Feel the heat radiating down into your feet and into your toes.

Notice the warm sensations throughout your body. How good it feels—so warm, so energizing. And somewhere in the back of your mind, there's a knowing, a gnawing sensation that your body's working more efficiently, more effectively than ever before. The pounds are dripping, dropping, falling, melting off of your body like butter on a hot summer's day.

HOT BEACH

Experience yourself standing on a hot sunny beach. The sun is just beating down upon you and it feels really good. You know how good it can feel to feel the hot sunrays penetrating your skin. It feels so good.

The sun is so hot that it heats up the sand beneath you to such an extent that the sand is reflecting the heat right back at you. It's as if you get a double effect, almost like being in an oven. It feels good to just stand on the hot sunny beach and bake in the hot sunshine.

Soon perspiration begins to form. It begins to form beads and the beads begin to form droplets and the droplets begin to form drops. The drops begin to drip, drip from your body. With each drop of perspiration, away drips toxins. Away drips calories. Away drips fat. Drip, drip, dripping away, melting away like butter on a hot summer's day. Yes, with each drop of perspiration, away drips toxins. Away drips calories. Away drips fat. Drip, drip, dripping away, melting away, like butter on a hot summer's day.

With each drop of perspiration, your body is becoming leaner and leaner and healthier. You can see, feel, imagine, notice, your body becoming leaner and leaner as each drop of perspiration drips away.

As you reach that body size that is just right for you, a cool breeze comes along and solidifies you right in that body size. Whenever you think of yourself, this is the way you think of yourself. A lean, healthy, fit individual.

Notice how your clothing fits your body. Perhaps you're wearing different clothing altogether. Notice how you move more easily, more freely, more quickly, more gracefully. You feel better about yourself and who you are—more confident. Others treat you differently, making positive comments about your lean, healthy, fit appearance.

Whenever you think of yourself, these are the kinds of thoughts and images you maintain. These good, healthy, thoughts and images of your lean, healthy, fit body. Any competing thoughts or images you banish from your mind. You replace them with these good healthy thoughts and images of your lean, healthy, fit body. For this is who you truly are. You are the kind of person who wears the kinds of clothing that you want to wear. Someone who moves easily and freely and gracefully—that's you. Someone who feels good about themself and who they are—that's you. Someone who others look to as a positive example—that's you. It feels good to think of yourself as a lean healthy individual.

Slim Feels

Nothing tastes as good as slim feels. Nothing tastes as good as slim feels. Nothing tastes as good as slim feels. And slim and fit and trim and healthy feels wonderful. Slim and fit and trim and healthy feels fantastic. Slim and fit and healthy feels amazing *all the time.* Something only tastes on the lips for a few brief moments and it's gone. But slim and fit and healthy feels fantastic *all the time:* every second of every minute, every minute of every hour, every hour of every day, every day of every week, every week of every month, month after month, year after year. Slim and trim and fit and healthy feels fantastic, all the time.

Nothing tastes as good as slim feels. Nothing tastes as good as slim feels. Nothing tastes as good as slim feels. And slim and fit and trim and healthy feels wonderful. Slim and fit and trim and healthy feels fantastic. Slim and fit and healthy feels amazing *all the time.* Something only tastes on the lips for a few brief moments and it's gone. But slim and fit and healthy feels fantastic *all the time:* every second of every minute, every minute of every hour, every hour of every day, every day of every week, every week of every month, month after month, year after year. Slim and trim and fit and healthy feels fantastic, all the time.

Nothing tastes as good as slim feels. Nothing tastes as good as slim feels. Nothing tastes as good as slim feels. And slim and fit and trim and healthy feels wonderful. Slim and fit and trim and healthy feels fantastic. Slim and fit and healthy feels amazing *all the time.* Something only tastes on the lips for a few brief moments and it's gone. But slim and fit and healthy feels fantastic *all the time:* every second of every minute, every minute of every hour, every hour of every day, every day of every week, every week of every month, month after month, year after year. Slim and trim and fit and healthy feels fantastic, all the time.

Nothing tastes as good as slim feels. Nothing tastes as good as slim feels. Nothing tastes as good as slim feels.

Sodas

There is something about sodas. And when I talk about sodas, I'm talking about regular sodas and diet sodas, or other kinds of sweetened drinks like Kool Aid or Slurpies or Slushies, or sweetened teas or even sweetened coffee drinks. I'm not at all referring to natural fruit juices. I'm talking more about the more processed kinds of sweet drinks, such as regular sodas or diet sodas, and other kinds of sweetened drinks like Kool Aide or Slurpies or Slushies, and even sweetened teas or sweetened coffee drinks. These sweetened drinks all have one thing in common and that is that none of them live up to what it is that they are supposed to do. That is, none of them are really thirst quenching or refreshing or satisfying. You know what I mean.

For, what happens is, the moment that sweet drink begins to enter into your mouth, it puts an obnoxious, sticky, sweet coating on your tongue and throughout the inside of your mouth. You know what I mean. As soon as that sweetened drink enters into your mouth, it puts an obnoxious, sticky, sweet coating on your tongue and throughout the inside of your mouth. Nothing will penetrate this obnoxious, sticky, sweet coating over your tongue and throughout the inside of your mouth. You can drink and drink that sweetened drink; however, you will never feel refreshed or satisfied or have your thirst quenched. All you are doing is dumping unwanted calories and preservatives into your body and you never will feel satisfied.

Only cool, clear, refreshing water will satisfy your thirst. You begin drinking some cool, clear, refreshing water and, as you do, it flows over your tongue and throughout the inside of your mouth, quickly rinsing away that obnoxious, sticky, sweet coating. It feels good to feel the cool, clear, refreshing water flowing over your tongue and throughout the inside of your mouth. It feels so refreshing, so satisfying, so thirst quenching. Only cool, clear, refreshing water satisfies you. It feels good to drink cool, clear, refreshing water.

WATER

There was a time when you were a youngster and you are playing outdoors at recess time and it's a hot day. Perhaps you're involved in some organized event like a ball game; or perhaps it's something more loosely organized like jumping rope or hopscotch, or playing on the jungle gym or teeter totter, or swinging on the swings; or maybe you're playing some running game like tag. It's a hot day and you know as youngsters how we become all involved in what we are doing and become oblivious to our own surroundings and even our own body functions.

Then something happens to summon you back to the schoolhouse. Perhaps the bell rings or a teacher blows a whistle or yells or in some other way summons everyone back to the schoolhouse. As you head back to the schoolhouse you begin to realize just how hot and dry and thirsty and parched you have become. You can feel the hot, dry, thirsty, parched sensations in your mouth. As you notice the hot, dry, sensations you begin thinking about the drinking fountain in the hallway. You pick up the pace and hurry back to the schoolhouse so that you can get to that drinking fountain in the hallway.

As you arrive at the drinking fountain in the hallway, you realize you are not the first one to have this idea. Yes, other youngsters have already lined up behind the drinking fountain in the hallway and you find your place at the end of the line. You're a bit anxious, because you don't know if there will be enough time for you to get a turn at the drinking fountain. Other youngsters are anxious as well and some of them are saying things to the person at the front of the line like, "Hurry up, we want a turn too," or, "Don't drink all of the water; save some for us." Perhaps someone gives that youngster at the front of the line a nudge of encouragement.

The longer you wait, the more certain you become that you will never get a turn at the drinking fountain. But it does become your turn and you grasp that cold faucet handle and you crank that water up. You begin sucking down that cool, clear, refreshing water as it hits your lips. You can feel that cool, clear, refreshing water flowing over your tongue and throughout the inside of your mouth. It feels so refreshing, so satisfying, so thirst quenching. It feels good to suck down gulp after gulp of cool, clear, clean, refreshing water. As you're sucking down gulp after gulp of cool, clear, clean, refreshing water, you're dreaming about being able to just stay at that drinking fountain forever and just suck down gulp after gulp of cool, clear, refreshing water, on and on forever.

Other youngsters are becoming anxious. They are saying things like, "Hurry up, we want a turn too," or, "Don't drink all of the water; we want some too." Perhaps someone from behind you gives you a nudge of encouragement; but you ignore their encouragements and continue sucking down gulp after gulp of cool, clear, clean, refreshing water. You continue dreaming about staying at that drinking fountain forever, and sucking down cool, clear, clean, refreshing water, on and on endlessly. It feels good to feel the cool, clear, refreshing water flowing over your tongue and throughout the inside of your mouth. It feels so refreshing, so satisfying, so thirst quenching. Nothing satisfies you like cool, clear, clean, refreshing water.

Then something happens to interrupt. The teacher is calling everyone back into the classroom. "It's time to clear the hall now. Everyone get back into the classroom." Even as you drag yourself away from that drinking fountain, you manage to get in those last few gulps of cool, clear, clean, refreshing water. As you walk back to the classroom you can feel the water sloshing around in your stomach. Back at your seat, you find yourself still dreaming about being at that water fountain forever and ever, sucking down cool, clear, refreshing water. It feels so good to feel the cool, clear, refreshing water flowing over your tongue and throughout the inside of your mouth. It feels so refreshing, so satisfying, so thirst quenching. Nothing satisfies you like cool, clear, refreshing water.

Pacing Chain around Control

[This script follows some pacing and leading or other suggestions.]

And, as a result, you feel more in control, and you are in control. And you are the kind of person who takes control in their life. I know this because you are listening to this [or because you came into my office today] and that's the sort of good, healthy, intelligent choice a person makes who takes control in their life. And more and more, every day in every way, those are the kinds of good, healthy, intelligent choices you find yourself making— those kinds of good, healthy, intelligent choices that put you in control. And who better to be in control of your life than you? Who knows your needs and wants better than you do?

Sometimes we get caught up in the daily business of being a good parent, or a good employee, or a good provider. Oftentimes we don't allow ourselves the time to just allow ourselves to reflect and ask, "What is it I really need out of life? What is it that will allow me to live life to the fullest, to feel fulfilled?" And, as a result, it becomes more and more apparent to you just what you do need and want out of life to feel more fulfilled, to live life to its fullest. Perhaps you find yourself taking some time out to just reflect, or perhaps it comes to you in the form of a dream, or perhaps it just becomes more apparent in your daily life. As a result, you find yourself setting good healthy boundaries. Yes, you set good healthy boundaries to get your needs met in a good healthy way. And, as a result of setting good healthy boundaries and getting your needs met in a good healthy way, you feel more in control. Not only do you feel more in control, you *are* in control. And who better to be in control of your life than you? When we are in control, we make good healthy choices—we gain freedom. No longer do we give away our control, no longer do we give away our choices. We gain freedom and when we are in control we feel more confident. We feel better about ourselves and who we are. And when we feel better about ourselves and who we are, good things just seem to happen. Perhaps you've noticed this before. Perhaps there have been times in your life when you felt confident and good about yourself and who you are, and good things just seemed to happen. It is a phenomenon that just occurs. There's no explaining it; it just happens that way.

And now, more and more, every day and in every way, you notice good things happening to you. More and more, you find yourself in the right place at the right time. More and more, you find those people and situations that you desire in your life, flowing into your life. More and more, good things just come to you. More and more, you notice the good things, the positive things. Every day good things, positive things, occur; and more and more, you find yourself focusing on the good things, the positive. Even on the worst day something good, something positive, occurs; and more and more, you find yourself focusing on the good, the positive. The more you notice the good, the positive, the more good positive things actually occur. It's a compounding effect. The more we notice it happening, the more it happens. More and more, you see the good, the positive, in every person and situation. More and more, you see the joy in life. More and more, you see the joy in your life. More and more, you notice the joy in every person and situation. As a result, for you the sun shines a little brighter. The sky is bluer. The grass is greener. The air is fresher. You walk with a new spring, a new bounce in your step. For you, stumbling blocks become stepping-stones. Yes, for you, stumbling blocks become stepping stones on the path of life, allowing you to see the path ahead more clearly, to move ahead more confidently, to move ahead more quickly; allowing you to see ahead into the future, knowing that good things are coming to you. Yes, things that were once problems you work through in a good healthy way; become strengths that you rely upon; strengths that allow you to move ahead into life with new confidence, a new boldness; taking on all that life has to offer with a new confidence, a new power. As a result, more and more, every day in every way, you feel better about yourself and who you are. You feel more alive, energetic and enthusiastic than the day before. The next time that you step outside into the air, and every time you step outside into the air, you notice a new energy, a new electricity, flowing through the air and into your body, causing you to feel alive, more energetic and enthusiastic. More and more, every day and in every way, you're better and better, looking forward to each new day and what it has to offer you.

SUGGESTIONS AROUND CONTROL
(SMOKING)

[This script follows other suggestion work, or deepening, or pacing and leading.]

More and more, you are in control. Yes, and you are someone who takes control. I know this because you came here today and that is the sort of action a person takes who takes control in their life. It's the sort of good, healthy, intelligent choice a person makes who takes control in their life. More and more, those are the kinds of choices you find yourself making more and more— those kinds of good, healthy, intelligent decisions that put you in control. And who better to be in control of your life than you? Who knows your wants and needs better than you do? Certainly not some weed rolled up in a piece of paper. No! Some weed rolled up in a piece of paper has no business controlling your life. From now on you take control. You make the choices.

You set good healthy boundaries. Yes, you set good healthy boundaries to get your needs met in a good healthy way. As a result of setting good healthy boundaries and getting your needs met in a good healthy way, you *feel more in control*. Not only do you *feel more in control, you are in control*. And who better to be in control of your life than you? Certainly not some weed rolled up in a piece of paper. No! Some weed rolled up in a piece of paper has no business controlling your life. From now on you make the choices. You take control. You make the choices that give you freedom—the freedom to live your life in the good healthy manner that you choose, no longer allowing some weed rolled up in a piece of paper to steal away your freedom. No! You take control. You choose freedom—the freedom to live your healthy new lifestyle in a way that you desire.

And when you're in control, you *feel more confident;* and when you *feel more confident,* you *feel better about yourself and who you are*; and when you *feel better about yourself and who you are,* good things just seem to happen. Perhaps you've experienced this before. Perhaps there was a time in your life when you felt confident and felt good about yourself and good things just seemed to happen. There's no explaining it; it's just a phenomenon that occurs. More and more now, every day in every way, you find good things happening to you. More and more, you find yourself in the right place at the right time. More and more, you find those people and situations that you desire in your life, flowing into your life.

More and more, you focus on the positive, the good, the healthy, the beneficial. More and more, you see the positive, the good, in every person and situation. Every day, good things, positive things, occur; and more and more, you focus on the good, the positive, the healthy, the beneficial. Even on the worst day something good, something positive, occurs. More and more, you experience the good, the positive, the healthy, the beneficial, in every person and situation.

Your new in-control lifestyle is a more positive lifestyle. You experience more freedom, more options; more opportunities come your way.

Suggestions around Control
(Food)

[This script follows other suggestion work or deepening.]

More and more, you are in control. Yes, and you are someone who takes control. I know this because you came here today and that is the sort of action a person takes who takes control in their life. It's the sort of good, healthy, intelligent choice a person makes who takes control in their life. More and more, those are the kinds of choices you find yourself making more and more—those kinds of good, healthy, intelligent decisions that put you in control. And who better to be in control of your life than you? Who knows your wants and needs better than you do? Certainly not food. No! Food has no business controlling your life. From now on you take control. You make the choices.

You set good healthy boundaries. Yes, you set good healthy boundaries to get your needs met in a good healthy way. As a result of setting good healthy boundaries and getting your needs met in a good healthy way, you feel more in control. Not only do you feel more in control, you are in control. And who better to be in control of your life than you? Certainly not food. No! Food has no business controlling your life. From now on you make the choices. You take control. You make the choices that give you freedom—the freedom to live your life in the good healthy manner that you choose. No longer do you allow food to steal away your freedom. No! You take control. You choose freedom—the freedom to live your healthy new lifestyle in a way that you desire.

And when you're in control, you *feel more confident;* and when you *feel more confident,* you *feel better about yourself and who you are;* and when you *feel better about yourself and who you are,* good things just seem to happen. Perhaps you've experienced this before. Perhaps there was a time in your life when you felt confident and felt good about yourself and good things just seemed to pop right into your life. There's no explaining it; it's just a phenomenon that occurs. More and more now, every day in every way, you find good things happening to you. More and more, you find yourself in the right place at the right time. More and more, you find those people and situations that you desire in your life, flowing into your life.

More and more, you focus on the positive, the good. More and more, you experience the positive, the good, in every person and situation. Every day, good things, positive things, occur; and more and more, you focus on the good, the positive, the healthy, the beneficial. Even on the worst day something good, something positive, occurs. More and more, you experience the good, the positive, the healthy, the beneficial in every person and situation.

Your in-control lifestyle is a positive lifestyle. You experience more freedom, more options; more opportunities come your way as a result.

CROSSROADS
(WEIGHT)

Experience yourself standing at a fork in the road. As you look down the fork that leads to the left, you notice it's a cold, barren, unfriendly road. This is the road of poor unhealthy choices. Along this road there are lots of food choices, although it's difficult to refer to these things as food, since they have so little nutritional value. Along this road is an abundance of junk food, sweets, sodas, fattening foods, foods high in refined carbohydrates, and all that you could possibly want.

What's missing from this road is that there are no hiking and biking trails; there are no mountains to climb, no rivers or lakes or streams to swim or boat or recreate in. There are no gyms or playing courts. There are, however, lots of big overstuffed couches and chairs. There are lots of TVs and VCRs and remote controls.

There is lots of clothing, like athletic wear for instance; however, it's the big baggy sweats—none of the formfitting active wear. There is everyday clothing as well, but it's more like big muumuus and things. Business wear, again, is the more over-sized loose fitting muumuus, certainly not the nicely tailored professional looking clothes. Eveningwear is again restricted to the big oversized choices, and there is the great big underwear as well.

This road, the road of poor unhealthy choices, also leads to illness and surgeries and a shortened life. There's time and opportunities that are missed with friends and family. There's an early death and time missed with children and grandchildren. It's a sad road.

As you turn from that road, you look down the right road. You see a beautiful road. The sun is shining brightly in a deep rich blue sky. The trees are full of leaves. The grass is green. The birds sing and the wildlife play in the fresh clean air. This is the road of good healthy choices. As you begin to walk down this road, you notice that there are all kinds of good healthy eating choices— lots of good, healthy, fresh fruits and vegetables growing right up out of Mother Earth, there for the picking. There are trees and bushes full of fruits and berries.

There are mountains to climb, rivers, lakes and streams to swim and boat and recreate in. There are lots of opportunities for exercise. There are gyms and tennis and racquetball and basket-ball courts and more.

There are lots of clothing options as well. There is athletic wear, the nice, formfitting kind that you would like to be seen in. There is everyday clothing like blue jeans and things, but, again, the more formfitting, form flattering kinds. Business wear is tailored and professional looking. With eveningwear there are lots and lots of options and, again, all the more tailored and formfitting kinds of things that you really want to wear.

This road, the road of good healthy choices, leads to a long happy life. It leads to opportunities and adventures. It leads to time to spend with friends and family, children, grandchildren and great-grandchildren.

Any time you make a choice about your lifestyle, whether it has to do with what you put in your mouth or the exercise that you do or don't get, then you are choosing one of these roads.

More and more, it feels good to choose the right road. The road of good healthy choices.

CROSSROADS
(SMOKING)

Experience yourself standing at a fork in the road. As you look down the road that leads to the left, you notice it's a cold, barren, unfriendly road—like an old black and white movie. The sky is dreary; a cold wind blows the mist and drizzle. The trees are barren of leaves. The grass has long been replaced by cold hard rock. This is the road of smoker. This road leads to pain, suffering and an early death. This is a sad road. It's cold, lifeless and dead.

As you turn from that road you look down the right road. You see a beautiful road. The sun is shining brightly in a deep rich blue sky. The trees are full of leaves. The grass is green. The birds sing and the wildlife play in the fresh clean air.

This is the road of a non-smoker. This road leads to a long, healthy, fit life. As you begin walking down this road, you feel a warm gentle breeze playing in your hair. With each step you feel healthier and healthier, stronger and fitter. As you walk further and further down this road, you know there is no way that any-one or anything could ever make you turn back to that cold unfriendly road of a smoker.

You choose life—the long healthy life of a non-smoker—for the rest of your life.

BODY PARTS

Perhaps you have some part of your body that you've become discouraged with. You might find yourself saying things like, "I hate my thighs," or, "I hate my stomach," or, "I hate my butt." Hate is not a healing emotion. These kinds of words and thoughts have only served to reinforce what it is that we don't want.

It's time to turn all that negativity around. It's time to start thinking of your body in a more positive way.

Imagine yourself holding that body part, holding it in your arms in the same manner that you would gently hold a baby. If that body part is your arms, that's fine. Just hold your arms in that manner. Experience yourself gently rocking and soothing that body part.

Experience yourself asking forgiveness for what you may have said or thought about it in the past. Now promise the body part that from now on you're only going to think and speak about it in the most nurturing, loving, positive ways.

BOOTSTRAPS

There is something I've noticed while working with you. It's that you possess a certain quality, something that not everyone has. It's a certain kind of tenacity, a toughness. I'll bet there was a time in your life when the world seemed to be coming down around you, a time when there wasn't someone around who could pick you up and help put things back together for you. It was one of those times when you just had to rely on yourself to put things back together and make your life work. It's one of those moments that I refer to as *picking yourself up by the bootstraps* and pulling things together and making it work, no matter what. You may know exactly what I'm referring to. It's not easy, but you make it happen.

Once we've had one of those bootstrap experiences, it gives us some inner wisdom, some character. From then on, somewhere in the back of the mind, we know that there is nothing that life can throw at us that we can't take on fully. We gain a certain inner strength, an ability to plow ahead no matter what. Not everyone possesses that ability. From then on we move ahead a bit more easily, a bit more confidently.

Perhaps now is a time when you need to use some of that *grab yourself by the bootstraps* energy and just know that you're moving ahead now, no matter what.

High Diving Board

Perhaps you recall as a youngster the first time you ever went off the high diving board. Maybe you had watched other youngsters jumping off and wished that you could do it to. Probably you found yourself walking near the high board and looking, sizing it up. Others may have teased you or dared you to try it.

Maybe you found yourself climbing the ladder, only to become scared and climb back down, perhaps many times. When you did get to the top maybe you froze, or found it difficult to walk out on the board or look down. If someone else came up the board, you might have stepped aside or climbed back down. Maybe you even felt embarrassed at times. Maybe others prodded you on. Perhaps you eased your way out to the end of the board a number of times looking down at the water below, only to move back away.

At some point, you found yourself standing at the end of the board, stepping out into space, trusting that gravity will do what it's supposed to do, and that the water will be there to do its job as well. Once you've stepped out into space there's no turning back. Suddenly you hit the water, perhaps there's a bit of sting and you're shooting down, down, deeper and deeper. The light at the surface gets further and further away. A new kind of fear begins to come over you as you begin to scramble to the surface.

As you break the surface, you gasp for air and exhilaration comes over you. You scramble to the edge and pull yourself up out of the water, breathing heavily, your heart pounding. You smile from ear to ear. Perhaps others are congratulating you.

Soon you find yourself at the top of the high board once again and you jump off more quickly now. Soon you are scrambling out of the pool and back up to the top of the high board, over and over again. What once was fear that held you back is now excitement. It feels exhilarating now.

GOAL

I can tell that you are the kind of person who knows how to set a goal. You are the kind of person who, when you put your mind to something, you achieve it. You know how to set goals and achieve them. I'll bet you set goals in your business life [*could add some client specifics here, like maybe you know they have sales quotas, etc.*] or in other areas. Sometimes, we set goals for things and don't even realize that is what we are doing. Most of us completed school and got a diploma. Sure, it may have seemed as though we didn't have much of a choice, but I'll bet that everyone thought of themselves getting that diploma and moving on to the next stage in life.

When we decide to go to college or trade school or even join the military, we have something long range in mind. Perhaps there was a time when someone thinks, "Gee, it might be nice to own my own home." As time goes on, what seemed to be a passing thought begins to make more and more sense. We might find ourselves dreaming about what kind of home we could afford, or what kind of neighborhood we might like to live in. Perhaps we begin putting away money for a down payment. We might find ourselves driving through potential neighborhoods. At some point, we might talk to a real estate agent or a mortgage lender. One day we find ourselves at a closing table receiving papers of ownership.

Maybe there was a time when you saw a place on TV, or in a magazine, or in the movies, and you thought something like, "Wouldn't it be nice to visit there?" As time goes by, that idea begins to take shape. Maybe you started looking at travel brochures and travel expenses. Maybe you started saving money and planning your schedule, until one day you find yourself in some exciting new place—all because you had some seemingly fleeting thought that developed into a goal that you achieved. The point is that most of us can and do set goals, even if we're not always aware that we are.

Sometimes we find it easy, even normal, to set goals for work or family. It can become normal to focus on those things and lose focus on ourselves and what we need. We don't often use our own abilities to achieve goals to just get our own needs met. It's easy, it seems, to put our own needs on the back burner. If we don't make ourselves a priority, where will we end up? Achieving all of those other things won't be possible if we're no longer around to make them happen.

We need to give ourselves the same sort of importance that we would to that next business project or community service, or whatever. What if you were to set goals for yourself and pursue them with the same tenacity that you pursue a project at work? What about that [workout routine/healthy eating/writing a book, *etc., etc.*] that has not been a priority?

More and more, doesn't it make sense to take better care of yourself?

Barnyard Fun

Now, I don't know if you've ever been in a barnyard. Lots of people have. Even people who have never been in a barnyard have a pretty good idea of what they might find there. Lots of different animals can be found in a barnyard, like goats or sheep or horses, even pigs. Mostly what people think of when they think of a barnyard are cattle. Cattle are probably the most common animals that we associate with a barnyard. Cattle eat a lot of grass and hay, and they drink lots of water. After they eat all of that grass and hay and drink all of that water, eventually it has to pass through their system. Wherever you find cattle in a barnyard, you find this substance that has passed through them. Now, this substance comes in a variety of shapes, sizes and consistencies. Now, some of this substance has a very high moisture content, so much so that it can't maintain any consistent shape and just flows wherever gravity takes it. Some of this substance still has a very high moisture content. Gravity still has an influence on it, but it has a bit more consistency, like mud. Some of this substance has a much lower moisture content and maintains a very consistent shape. Some of this substance is very dry; however, it maintains a very consistent shape, although any contact with it would easily break it up. There is yet more that is very dry and has no consistent shape at all, more like sawdust. This is the consistency we are interested in. This consistency is like that stuff in cigarettes. In fact, it's the same as that stuff in cigarettes.

Just experience yourself gathering up some of this substance [manure/cow shit, *etc.*] and roll it up in a piece of paper. And now light the end of that paper. You can smell that smell. Burning manure has got to smell horrible, and you can smell that smell. As you put that smoldering manure cigarette up to your face, your nose begins to burn and itch and run. Your eyes begin to